To Ted ~~Winkelmeyer~~
on his 17th
birthday from
his uncle,
Robert K. Winkelmey-
10-19-'67.

THIS DOUBLE THREAD

THIS
DOUBLE
THREAD

Walter Starcke

HARPER & ROW, PUBLISHERS

NEW YORK, EVANSTON, AND LONDON

FIRST EDITION

LIBRARY OF CONGRESS CATALOG CARD NUMBER: 67-14937

FR

. . . lay hold on me fully, both by the
Within and the Without of myself,
grant that I may never break this
double thread of my life.

—PIERRE TEILHARD DE CHARDIN
from *The Divine Milieu*

Contents

PREFACE   ix

PART I

THE DEVELOPMENT OF A MODERN MYSTICISM

CHAPTER

1 · The Condition of Man   I

2 · The Ultimate Man and Today   8

3 · The Maze and the Map   22

4 · The Old and the New   33

5 · The Search and the Secret   44

6 · To Love Another   53

7 · The Greatest Commandment   62

PART II

THE APPLICATION OF A MODERN MYSTICISM

8 · The Play and the Plot   71

9 · The Serpent's Trick and the Great Lie   83

10 · The What and the How   97

11 · The Now and the How   109

12 · A Matter of Life and Death   119

13 · The Triune Way   130

14 · The Cup of Life   140

Preface

Like most of us, I was thrust into this explosive century ill equipped to understand or cope with it. I had no more lofty motive than to just keep afloat, if possible to be creative and reasonably happy. I felt it would be nice to be important and respected, even to be a noble soul contributing to the betterment of mankind, but every bit of my frantic energy was spent in just surviving and in appliquéing some kind of mask over what I considered my inadequacy.

My early years were almost a cliché of the typical American boy, with typical American home life, followed by the typical American college experience. But World War II pulled the blinds off of a lot of colored glass innocence, and, innocent or not, I was left to reap the results of my confusion.

I was twenty-four years old, and my goal up to this point had been to experience everything I could, to leave no stone unturned. I had, perhaps, a more than typical appetite to experience everything I was exposed to, and the chapters in my soap opera covered every kind of personal relationship, at least a sample of every taste, every indulgence on the market.

I arrived in New York at the end of the war not only shaken by the experience of having been part of the war machine, but also devastated within by my personal and moral chaos; my health shattered as well. I was about as full of holes as a sieve, and felt there was not enough time or even the possibility of getting the holes plugged up by psychiatry or anything else. My only chance, it seemed, was to find one central answer behind life to cling to.

I began to search through the important scriptures of the world's major religions in the hope of finding some threads that attained credibility by appearing in them all. I was desperate. I could not accept anything that did not make sense, nor was there any space for the excess baggage of spiritual theorems that did not apply to my daily life.

The search led me to extended stays in Hindu monasteries, visits to Europe and the Orient, around the world, for that matter, in quest of every person or place that could reveal another missing piece to the puzzle. Above all, I was determined not to accept anything that I had not experienced myself, or that I did not have reason to believe in time I could make part of my life and experience.

It would be inaccurate to call this a religious search in the light of the limited meaning we usually assign to the word religion, though it would be accurate to say I searched religiously. I not only investigated many forms of meditation and mantra, but also participated in all other levels of life. The aesthetic level took me into the fields of art and the theater, into the principles of the creative processes. Next, it was obvious that any answer of value had to work in the market place as well as in theory or be relegated to the area of the old-fashioned religious palliative; so I participated in the world of finance and business. Actually I was not turning my back on any of the aspects of life that had backfired for me before, but I was searching for the principles which would make for a life lived harmoniously, constructively, healthily, and fully at the same time.

First my own physical condition and well-being changed and transformed in extraordinary manner, revealing that though I wasn't setting the attainment of health as my goal, a process which made for a more comfortable and creative life was taking place. I couldn't fail to see that something had to be right, as a degree of material success and public recognition came in each field of endeavor.

At first I thought that the success was despite my private search for the truths of life. But I soon came to realize that the material rewards were the effects; the cause was the search and the principles I discovered on the way.

I found that those who were driven by a passion for finding, whether their searches took them to the bars of Skid Row, or up the blind alleys of way-out metaphysical cults, came closer to attaining something than those who sat frozen in the polished pews of the past.

For me, life itself has been the temple. Therefore, the toughest job I have had has been in refusing to live life falsely because of what others might think, or because of what my mind claimed I "should" do in its attempt to keep me under its domination. There have been years of aloneness when everything in me begged me to accept the fact that I was nothing but a phony and a fool. But, frankly, I didn't have any choice in the matter, because I knew I had to live, and that I couldn't live with personal hypocrisy, with the refuge of conformity, or a double standard.

Fortunately, I met two men as I began this journey whose influence on me was eternally profound. One was my guide in all external matters. From him I learned much of the meaning of artistic integrity and human appreciation, of the arts, theater, and the exquisite potential of the material world. That was John van Druten whose last three plays I produced on Broadway.

The other was Joel Goldsmith, whose writings compose one of the most lucid examples of pure mysticism we have for the modern man in this age. With the consciousness, language, and symbols of the West he combined the values of the East, and upon the foundation of his teaching and association my own journey was based.

As I neared my late thirties, after some fifteen years of search that was often rewarding but that never guaranteed an ascertainable fulfillment, I found myself sick with some strange fever, alone, in Ceylon, the end of the road to the farthest corner of the world. In this moment of a more total emptiness than ever before, a breakthrough took place within. It was like that wonderful moment when one is putting together a jigsaw puzzle and out of the chaos a recognizable pattern reveals itself. There were still lots of pieces to fit into the puzzle, but now I knew where I was going. Things were never quite the same. The panic was never quite as disturbing, the problems never quite as unsolvable, the vision never again obliterated.

This book is the revelation of the pieces of my puzzle. To say it is complete would be to limit the picture and I, for one, hope the picture is never totally complete because I want to live life fully. In this book I am offering the pattern to my puzzle, not as a suggestion that the reader's can be the same, for there are no two exactly alike. There can be striking similarities, however, and perhaps some of my tips, some of my road signs, can give an idea of how life operates for me. I am not proposing a system, creating a religion, nor am I denouncing anyone else's conclusions or beliefs.

I have no halo, tarnished or otherwise, and my clay feet are right out in front of me, easy to spot. But this is the most exciting day in the history of mankind and I would rather jump into it on my clay feet, which have brought me excitedly and happily this far, ready to participate at all levels of this infinite experience of life, than to dry-up waiting to find less vulnerable feet on which to stand.

If you care to join me, there is one thing I would like to ask of you. It takes a conscious effort to check old concepts in order to assimilate new ones. Unfortunately, we have to communicate mostly with words, and every word is burdened with a thousand different connotations. At best we can redefine old words in an attempt to find a common ground of understanding. Face to face we can repeat, redefine, rephrase, reevaluate until a rapport is achieved. The impersonal medium of the written word bars such exchange; so I ask that you make as strong an effort as possible to free yourself of your prejudged views.

Words such as "spirit," "love," "truth," "God" may be understood in one way by some and evoke in them a response of violent antagonism while others may respond to the same words with a different interpretation, resulting in a feeling of joy and peace. But, as words are man-made they are man-twisted, and we have come to realize that they most often mean exactly the opposite of what they claim. One is immediately wary of a car dealer who calls himself "Honest John" because the hypocrisy of such a label almost assures the reverse. Through the centuries, man has done more killing in the name of love than in any other. He has lied in the name of truth and used the word "God" to excuse his most selfish and demonic ends.

It is natural that anyone who has been burned by the hypocrisy of man would try to reject all words that expect him to have faith and hope in that which he cannot see and touch with his own hands. But just as the mathematician must accept an unknown quantity called x in order to arrive at a solution to his problem, we must have the strength to see and use some of the old words if we expect to gain some comprehension of the abstract or less visible levels of life.

It would be ideal to have a whole new set of fresh unconditioned words to play with, but that cannot be. So I have decided not to pussyfoot around in an attempt to avoid dangerous or hypocritically conditioned words, but rather simply to explain my use of them and to ask for that usage of my meanings, unpedantically.

One might believe that it is more difficult for those who have rejected the words "truth," "life," "love," and "God" to accept a new use for them than for those who have already accepted the words. That is not true. Those who have turned against the common usage of the words are free to accept new meanings; those who already accept them have the almost impossible job of getting free from their accepted concepts in order to see the words in a new light. No matter how hard they try they automatically assume the author sees the words as they do.

It is the aim of this writing, as it is the aim in all communication, to find a common ground of understanding as a bridge from the seeable, touchable, tastable material world to the principle, idea, or thought that brought it into being.

PART I *The Development of a Modern Mysticism*

❧ ❧

CHAPTER 1

THE CONDITION
OF MAN

❧

Changes are taking place at all levels of life. They have always taken place, but in the past the advance has been slow and even controllable. Today the rate of change has assumed the speed of a geometric progression, and the noise of change has reached a crescendo. To anyone with his ears open this noise sounds the call note of a new day.

Perhaps the single most significant and dramatic announcement to the world that this new day is at hand was made the moment man succeeded in splitting the atom. In preatomic time, despite speculation about the realm of the spiritual, the material world was right at fingertips and it seemed evident that ultimate security lay in matter. On the foundation of this belief society became structured. As this basis of society has continued until today, many still feel they can find protection in guns, money in the bank, social institutions, and governments. With the splitting of the atom, this central, heretofore indestructible fact—the predictable security of matter—has been replaced. The startling revelation is that the splitting of the atom announces the arrival of what might be called the spiritual day, because the supreme power of materiality has once and for all been exposed as vulnerable to the power of something within man's mind and spirit.

The hazard is that when the kingpin to which a society relates is challenged or removed, the entire society may become numbed or rendered immobile. A classic example was found in both ancient Mexico and Peru. In both of those societies the arrival of a handful of Spanish soldiers was of such significant importance as to cause those whole nations of many millions of population to stand still. The Spaniards did not overcome those civilizations by the power of arms. The countries defeated themselves. Their God King, their concept of supreme power, was destroyed when a more mysterious and greater power arrived wearing shining armor and riding on strange animals. The populace simply sat down. Institutions ceased to function, for the kingpin which held everything together was removed.

This isn't as farfetched from our modern day as it may seem. When President Kennedy died, much of the world went immobile for several days, and his death was only the end of a single man, not the end of a whole system.

But our whole system of society was challenged when the supremacy of materiality was challenged. The underpinnings are being removed one by one as the result of this cardinal fact. There are many who notice the rapidity of the changes taking place and who sense that the systems invented by man are not going to sustain society much longer in its present form.

It is hard to imagine, but if the average man were told that his survival depended on his starting immediately to communicate at some entirely unaccustomed level—a level of vibration, for instance—or that he had to hear that which he couldn't hear, see that which he couldn't see, he would panic.

Now that thinking man realizes he cannot look to the phenomenal world for absolute security, he must find it in another way, at another level. Sensing that the changes in our social structure may relegate our existing society into immediate obsolescence, many are turning to the other than phenomenal world—the invisible and absolute. By mistaking the psychic and occult for the nonphenomenal world, many have indulged in attempts at misguided mysticism. On the other hand, there are those who have wanted to break through the limitations of the finite surface world of objects and have concluded that psychedelic drugs are the answer. They believe that since these drugs affect the mind, they may induce an experience beyond the experience of known phenomenal existence.

Understanding Those of the New Generation

If we want to understand the young people born after the atomic event, it is necessary to realize that most of our young have been raised during a time when the old acceptance of, or value placed on, the material constitutes an insult to the mind.

Today it is often heard that the young people do not seek the goals of the past, that they have no direction or purpose. Perhaps this is because the standards by which we once valued those goals have been changed. The goals no longer carry a desire potent enough to motivate the young into exerting the energy necessary or into finding the direction needed to achieve them.

The mythical panacea of accumulating a million dollars, the promised rewards for achieving public fame, the lure of being thought well of by fellow man are yardsticks that measure nothing of value any longer. The rise in the use of psychedelic drugs and other mind-manipulating agents is a yardstick indicating where many are looking, in a completely different direction, for fulfillment of their desires.

Alarmed over the rising use of drugs, many persons, groups, and institutions are attempting to change the pattern by legislation or by compiling and publishing frightening reports of the harmful effects of the use of drugs. Such attempts are a bit naïve. No change in the pattern will be made until it is understood just why people are turning to drugs, what causes the initial desire, and what they expect to get from them.

Many of the young first sample psychedelic drugs because they are told that through them they can experience something beyond the familiar phenomenal level. They want that experience partly because they sense, perhaps more clearly than those whose values were formed in the preatomic day, that there is no security in the phenomenal level. They know they must relate to another level if they expect to fulfill the natural desire in man to find security somewhere. The young instinctively investigate any avenue hinting that it will lead to an expansion of consciousness that will bring a new awareness of life free from material limitations.

The choice of clothing and music, or the behavior of many of the rebellious young is not accidental or unrelated to their desire for freedom from the limitations of the object world. They reason that if one has need only for the shirt on his back and a single pair of pants he is free from the fear of dependence upon material security. No one can harm him by taking away what he does not possess.

In the case of their desire for love or even sexual relationship, for that matter, they feel they can find security or at least freedom from hurt in one of two ways. By attempting to love a number of different people, no devastating loss can follow should any one individual drop out of their lives or walk out on them. The other way to be safe is to love no one at all.

Often the excesses of conduct are no more than desperate attempts to break through the sound barrier, to relate to the nonobjective or to what one might even call the mystical. No one can denounce that motive, nor the desire to find a way to function in this changing world. The trouble lies not so much in the motive as in the methods used.

It has been said that in a generation everyone will probably take some form of hallucinogenic agent such as LSD or marijuana with the same aplomb and frequency with which the public now nibbles aspirins and tranquilizers, or sips alcohol. The use of drugs to attain an "other world" experience is not new. Many Oriental religious orders have for centuries experimented with drugs in order to induce inner experiences; none of them, however, has found the solution through this method, none has established utopia—or mankind would long ago have reached fulfillment. Yet, if one were to say that in a generation all of mankind will be able to find release from the pressures of the phenomenal world, he might be right. But when that day arrives as a possibility for the majority of mankind, as it has for a few in the past, there will be no need for the use of external agents. That freedom, if it is to be true and complete freedom, must come from the source that is within each individual. Then the desire will be satisfied, as it can be, in a natural way.

The Day of Mysticism

When one talks about the reality of the mystical or of mysticism it brings forth an immediately negative response in the minds of most sophisticated or down-to-earth people today. And understandably so. There have been so many raffish escapist practices that have been called mystical. There has been so much idol-worshiping religious asceticism equated with mysticism. There most certainly also have been a number of people who have found a way to escape from life by withdrawing from the world, calling themselves mystics, and letting others take care of their human needs. Commenting on this kind of escape act, Aldous Huxley once said, "Anyone can be a mystic on ten thousand a year."

But let us take a fresh look at the meaning of the word. The dictionary says mysticism is "the doctrine that the knowledge of reality, truth, or God is attainable by direct revelation" and that it is the attempt to identify with the source of all life and being. It is the desire to relate to the absolute, to transcend finite limitations, to realize the ultimate cause behind life.

In that respect nothing could be more practical than being a mystic. Nobody needs to claim that mysticism necessitates copping out on life or separating from the world of men. In fact, it requires exactly the opposite. It means knowing life and the principles of life more profoundly. All great artists and all creative people in no matter what field have brought forth their creations by tapping the source of life. The more successfully man tunes in to the source, getting right to the truth of things, the more productive he will be.

All those who are seeking to look beyond appearances to find a better way to create, all those who are trying to delve into the invisible secrets behind success, all those who have ever tried to understand the supernatural, all those who are trying to relate to the nonphenomenal—in order to better understand the phenomenal and better survive in this changing and challenging day—might be surprised to hear themselves called mystics, but that is what they are.

CHAPTER 2

THE ULTIMATE
MAN AND TODAY

If man did not have the instinctive belief that there is an ultimate good or some evolving advancement for man he wouldn't attempt to discover new truths, invent new instruments for the betterment of man, or pierce the invisible. Almost everyone would like to believe in good, that mankind has made progress over the years, and that there is an ultimate purpose behind life. Otherwise there is nothing left for man but a futile race on the treadmill. As his power diminishes, he finally loses the ability even to stay in one spot.

In the face of the high pitch that man's inhumanity to man has reached in this century, it takes a great talent for seeing two sides of a situation not to lose sight of the advancements man has made. We must remember, if we want to keep some balance in the picture, that it was only yesterday when enslavement was common practice, when the mentally sick were persecuted in dungeons. Just a few years ago the wealthiest of men stank from filth and did not clean themselves. Only yesterday there was no such thing as recreation or taking vacations, and the great mass of mankind had to spend every waking moment simply taking care for the bodily needs. Only a few hundred years ago knowledge was the exclusive privilege of the aristocracy and the clergy, and all the rest could neither read nor write. Then the printing press was invented, making knowledge available to the mass of mankind and from that invention man learned about freedom and individual rights. The release from the bondage of ignorance seems so remote to us today that we cannot imagine what the world was like in those days. Even today, already the atom is being used to create electric power. In 1966 over half of the new electric plants constructed that year were using atomic energy, and before long all the new plants will be using it. Already the atom is being harnessed to turn salt water into man's most necessary element, fresh water. It would be hard to keep from realizing that now there are truths at our fingertips that will free mankind from more and more of his limitations, in areas impossible for us even yet to conceive.

Those who, with the tools of currently available knowledge, have penetrated the past and related it to the present no longer have to accept a positive progress of mankind by an act of blind faith. No matter in what field a person may be interested, the smallest amount of research reveals to him new techniques and new advances. To refuse to acknowledge an advancement for mankind would be like a moth trying to cling to its dark cocoon, unable to imagine the liberation to come when it is free to fly in the sunlight.

Evolution of Man

Anthropologists have been showing us how man has been evolving over the years. They tell us that since the first single-cell life, the direction has been toward increasing dimension, complexity, and sophistication. Amorphous amoebic life assumed definite shape and size. Locomotion evolved. Each new extension necessitated more complicated physical machinery. A kind of unconscious intelligence evolved to activate and perpetuate this machinery. Each evolvement represented a greater advance, a greater expression of consciousness, a greater capacity for truth.

This mental and physical sophistication reached its high point of refinement when it became personalized as man. There was a development in man that separated him from all other animals. The power of intellect or mind in man became strong enough to dominate his physical passions and drives. At a zoo we feel compassion for the apes or other higher forms of animal life when they show us how close they are to having this human faculty. We say, "Oh look, he is almost human," when we see an animal approximate human control, and in a way we feel sad as we watch the animal's struggle for this added dimension. It is even more saddening to watch our fellow man struggling to put more distance between his animal passions and his desire to live among his fellow beings as a free intelligent person. Nevertheless, when man's mind grew strong enough to control his animal desires he could resist the temptation to steal his neighbor's food, to take his neighbor's wife, or to destroy his neighbor's home in a fit of physical anger. He found he was not limited to living alone but could form tribes, communities, and ultimately nations where a greater good for all could be accomplished by cooperation.

When there was only animal existence, one side, the physical side, was dominant, but the second side, the mental side, was actually evolving along with the physical. With the advent of the power of mind to dominate the body it became the more potentially powerful.

Though the two were inseparable, they were distinct and individual. Though one could see and touch the body, the power of the invisible mind was real and material in that it was visible as both the body and as the bodily performance it directed.

After many centuries it became evident that a third side was evolving. This faculty had to do with consciousness itself, with man's ability to discern or sense the impersonal essence of the spiritual ground of being—the spiritual faculty. This evolving spiritual faculty manifested itself in ever more sophisticated religious expression, from the simple recognition that there was some invisible spirit like truth in the elements of sun and water that perpetuated life, through the multiple gods signifying the many aspects of human need, to the belief in a single all-inclusive God embracing all the spirit of truth and life.

History began to be marked by the examples of individual men whom society had singled out as being more spiritually advanced than others. At least something was different about them. There were invisible aspects to their nature that made them a bit more free than others, a bit more in control of the fears and passions that drove other men. The high point of this spiritual development in the Oriental man was found in the evolvement of Gautama the Buddha. In the West, spiritual evolvement expressed itself in the life of a man called Jesus of Nazareth.

The First Whole Man

The world over, there is as much conditioned response, reaction, and one-sided vision attached to the name Jesus as there is to any other, perhaps more so. But for the purpose of this present exploration let us check all other beliefs and see Jesus as a man representing a very significant development, a very significant moment in history.

It might shock some to hear it put so bluntly, but Jesus

fits the description the dictionary gives for a "mutation."
It tells us that a mutation is "a sudden, well-marked
transmissible variation in the organism of an animal or
plant. A sudden departure from the hereditary background, as when an individual differs from its parents." As
such, a mutation is not only an extraordinary happening
when a new form becomes created but it is also marked
by the fact that the new form can be followed by others,
that it establishes a whole new being. Jesus not only represented something new for mankind but also he revealed
a new dimension that all those who followed him could
have.

The advent of Jesus marks the most important event in
the history of man on earth because his life marks the
moment when the third or spiritual faculty in man
evolved into fulfillment and was transmissible for all those
who came afterward, or, at least, potentially transmissible. When we look at it in this light, there can be no doubt
that mankind's adulation of the birth of Christ is justi-
fied.

If Jesus is the first recognized product of this high point
of evolution, mankind's acceptance of Jesus as the first
begotten offspring of the ultimate truth of being is ap-
preciated. Man's inability to comprehend the significance of this evolvement blinded him to the words of
Jesus when, over and over again, he said that this possibility was within each one of us. He said that we should all
have greater freedom; that we could be in the earth but,
through the expansion of this new sense, we would be free
from the bondage that man had lived under before that
time—just as, when mind developed, man was greatly
freed from the limitations under which the animals lived.
Jesus said that man had that within him which could give
him freedom even over death.

Though Jesus was the first man known to be born with
the capacity for full spiritual realization, even he, symbol-

ically or otherwise, did not evolve to the fullness of this capacity until about the time he started his public ministry. Then his physical, mental, and spiritual capacities joined in demonstrating his consciousness of some greater truth of life by his transcendence over matter and by his degree of inner freedom and peace. With all sides developed he became the first example we have of a totally free, totally whole, man.

The Three Powers

None of the three aspects of man—body, mind, and spirit—should contradict the others, none should conflict, none compete. They do not in a whole man. Each has its own power and its own use. The power of the body is in its physical senses that respond to the material world and in its physical capacity to house, transport, and carry out the orders of the other faculties. When a man is in a state of poise, his body does not struggle against his mind or spirit.

The power of the mind lies in its ability to articulate inner feelings, to retain knowledge, to communicate, to reason, and also to instruct and balance the body. There are many other uses for the power of the mind, but there are also many limitations, and the mind has played many tricks on man in order to claim that *it* is the most important side of man.

Early civilizations in Egypt felt that by mummifying the human body men could perpetuate the physical existence and preserve its life for all eternity. Man now feels that if he can preserve his ideas he can preserve and perpetuate his mind. To try to limit truth through human concepts is man's attempt to make the human mind the greatest power. But to abandon the search for truth, to abandon the desire to live life from the spiritual source within, constitutes victory for the mind. To continue to expect to find truths to use, to expect to find some power that produces happiness and prosperity is a victory for the mind when that expectation implies that the mind will have ever more power within itself. When the mind thinks that it can collect a lot of knowledge to use as a power over life, it is struggling to be supreme in power. The paradox that has reached its most devilish reality today is that our new spiritual capacities strengthen the mind with each new truth they reveal, yet ultimately the spirit must harness the mind.

Those who proclaim the importance of the human mind, of understanding, of realizable knowledge are correct as long as they acknowledge the equal importance of the other aspects of man's nature. Those who are not aware of the danger of the tyranny of mind miss the fact that ultimately freedom is found not only by the mind, but mainly through the spirit. True and profound inner or spiritual revelation that one senses from within never insults intelligence nor the body, but it transcends them both.

A few since the time of Jesus, and probably a number of whom the world has no knowledge, have attained a high degree of fulfillment. Yet they have been unable mentally or physically to communicate more than glimpses of it because it is as impossible to translate spirit into intellect as it is to translate intellect into the terms of bodily function. How could one explain thinking to an animal? How could one explain color to a person born without sight?

Since the beginning of any spiritual development in man, mystics have struggled with this impossibility and have found that it is perhaps possible to lift one into the spirit by the spirit, but not by the intellect alone. Yet the mind keeps struggling to understand, because the spiritual faculty is pushing within. The mind is of little help and often much of a hindrance, just as the body is a hindrance to the mind. The body seeks physical fulfillment, and the mind transcends this physical desire.

The evolution of the mind as power did not grow by fighting bodily power but rather grew alongside it. Man's spiritual faculty will not grow through fighting the mind. Many in the Orient and some in the Western world have made the mistake of believing that they could bludgeon the mind into submission. The practice of enforced celibacy and monastic austerity are attempts to discipline the body and mind into submission with the goal of developing the spiritual faculty. In this the Buddhists did not listen to the illustrious Buddha who, after he had attained enlightenment, condemned the practice of extreme austerity. The spiritual power grows beside body and mind, and the less we do to fight mind or body, the better.

The power of the spiritual dimension is the source of man's ability to create. The other two dimensions, body and mind, are necessary for the creative faculty to fulfill itself, but the ability to sense the unformed and bring it into being is a unique capacity of spirit. Animals cannot create new forms. They can instinctively build homes and nests, basically the same year after year, and they can procreate their species, but they cannot create new forms. That is why it is said that man is made in the image of God. God is creativity and man can create.

The simplest way to describe the power of spirit is that its power lies in the power of imagination. It might seem flippant to use such a commonplace word as imagination to help explain the spiritual, but look at what a very important position it has in our daily lives. The most mundane act of creativity could not occur without imagination. First comes the idea and later it is followed by the form. A housewife decides to bake a cake. She envisages it or imagines it. Next, her mind is used to list the needed ingredients. Then her hands mix them. And finally the cake appears in form on the table. Her whole being was needed, but the most important single creative moment was when she imagined the cake.

The same activity of imagination takes place in any creation whether in the enormously productive world of the businessman, the engineer, the scientist, or the artist —first the imaging, then the execution, and finally the form. The success or failure of the form depends on the good or bad imaging and execution.

Perhaps the opening line of the book of St. John is not so esoteric or secretive as we once thought, "In the beginning was the word." In the beginning there is always the word, thought, idea. This word, thought, or imaged idea was the creative action. Then the idea gave birth to all things; no thing is created without the imagination.

In ignorant man this power of imagination is as dangerous as an atom bomb in the hands of a barbarian. Everything that exists in the world of form is imagination externalized, formed. This power of imagination can externalize itself in destruction as well as in beauty and creation. What is more, this force of imagination is never inactive while man is conscious. Just as we are never without our bodies or our minds, we are never without our imaginations. As we walk down the street we are either imaging negatively or positively. When we run into someone we dislike we are tempted to negative imaging and thereby we perpetuate the negative. When we encounter a friend, the force that images friendliness not only increases the friendship but warms us with a personal glow. If we want to change the form of our lives, therefore, then we must alter this source of creation within us, our imaginations. By the same token, anything that stimulates the imagination in such a way that we lose control of our own imaging should be viewed with circumspection. An uncontrolled imagination can open a Pandora's box of distortion that may be followed by visible results. But, when the imagination is healthy and in control, when the body is healthy and strong, when the mind is trained and developed, we can be whole persons, fully evolved and creative.

A Kind of Faith

Each aspect of the whole man is a completely different sense (body sense, mind sense, spiritual sense). As none of these can really take the place of the others, so it requires a kind of an act of faith for each of the senses to cooperate with the others. Every act of creation takes place only when the imagined idea manifests itself in coordinated form by an act of faith.

Every time we drive a car we do so having faith that the car passing just a few feet away will not suddenly head into us; every time we turn a switch we have faith that light will come; and every second our faith in the body of mankind is reaffirmed whether we know it or not. The man who claims to be an atheist denies atheism from the moment he believes the sun will rise to the time he drinks a glass of milk, having full faith that it is certified and healthy.

Yet behind these acts of faith are logical reasons that it is now possible for the human mind to know and accept. In this century, however, there are examples of some of the most developed intellects who are nonetheless trapped by their minds because they are unable to accept fully anything which their facile minds cannot totally digest and encompass. They are tricked by the necessity to dot every "i" and cross every "t."

There are certainly great lapses of logic in the word made flesh of the Christian message, in the consciousness expressing itself in the form. There is hardly any recognizable logic in the advice given in the Sermon on the Mount that if someone sues you for your cloak, give him also your coat, for quite obviously it is logical that you would then freeze to death. Indeed, modern science has found its most important breakthroughs by deliberately starting with an illogical premise; by starting from what have heretofore been impossible results and by working back, the key has been found to open miraculous understanding.

Man in his weakness can superstitiously accept invisibles through fear. Man in his strength can also accept invisibles when he is secure enough in himself not to dread his demise should he step out occasionally into the unknown. At times it is spiritually wise to be foolish.

The first faltering step into a conscious realization that man operates at many levels beyond the senses, beyond the visible, is necessary. Less evolved man was scared into the step through fear of the unknown. Today, more advanced man is finding the step increasingly easier because science's staggering inventions testify to the actual dimensions of the invisible. Even those who are taking faltering steps toward a belief in occult mysticism, in fortunetelling, in visitors from other planets are opening themselves to areas apart from the phenomenal. The desire in the young to believe in flying saucers is their instinctive realization of nonphenomenal existence, of faith in the invisible.

Some of the young are turning to the use of LSD or marijuana because they wish an escape from a world where the logical powers of the reasoning mind are out of balance with the other aspects of life. They desire to step out into that "fertile void" where sensing and feeling are not so mentally controlled. They want to have faith in something that is not visible. When they realize that the attainment of this third dimension is a natural and present development in man they will not get sidetracked. By attaining the third level of consciousness naturally the valuable instrument of the mind is not harmed or insulted, abdicated or rendered uncreative. It is used rather to create the whole man.

The Whole Person and the Measuring Stick

In childhood, discovery of the body and fascination with the material world occupies most of the child's awareness. During the teen years one not only experiences the physical world, but one also begins to explore its mental and physical secrets. The very growth of the body and its new powers are taking place daily before the eyes of the young adult. The arrival of sexual drives and impulses puts a new light on all relationships and activities. This whole new aspect of life has to be coped with, understood, and directed. After these levels are explored, the time comes when the importance of spiritual or inner realities begins to assert itself in the natural drive toward balance. To expect or want the young to concentrate on the spiritual side before the other sides are discovered and developed is not realistic or even advisable.

Naturally, a total lack in any area portends a problem of future balance and no side can be fully understood or developed if the other sides are totally left out, but the emphasis on the body-mind levels that are instinctive in the early years prepares a platform for the proper equation of spiritual development in its own time and season.

To try to force on the young what the adult thinks is the proper emphasis on the spiritual, because it is for him in his own stage of progress, can be not only wrong but harmful. It is necessary for each side to be given its chance to develop fully. If one is curtailed in his concentration in one area before the goal is reached, it may flaw future development.

Some young adults are ready to concentrate on the spiritual earlier than others or even to reverse the process. No one can say it is not worthy for the young to be spiritual-minded, yet no one can say it is a virtue either unless they can behold the whole being, not in terms of any single moment of time, but rather in knowledge of the whole development. To grow into a whole man all three aspects must be developed and balanced, and then man will attain the freedom of being a whole person.

There is a kind of measuring stick we can use that will either help us grow into a whole person, or will help us maintain our wholeness after we have found it. In any endeavor we approach, any activity, any relationship, we can ask ourselves, "Can I take my whole self into this experience?"

In all personal, business, and even romantic relationships, if one is taking just his body into the experience, and possibly his mind, but not his spirit, it is destined to be a limited if not poisonous relationship. When one is prepared to take his whole self into a relationship the chances are that it will be a rewarding and healthy one. Even if one is approaching a relationship for which no long duration is anticipated, the test of whether to proceed or not is measured by this yardstick. When single men or women meet a new person who interests them, they do not have to wonder about next week or next month. If the encounter passes the test they can at least know the next move. If they feel they can take their minds and their spirits into the relationship as well as their physical selves, it has a foundation on which to stand. If there is no communication of spirit or mind, it is a lopsided relationship. If one can take his whole self along, it is an honest move at the start.

When one approaches a new job or profession taking only his mind and body into it but not his real interest, heart, or spirit, it is destined to be a frustrating and debilitating experience.

When one entertains the idea of a philosophical or religious activity, it will be fruitless if it insults the mind. By the same token, one should not enter upon a religious activity or go into church without being prepared to take his body into it. The body of man is not just his physical aspect; it is also his physical expression of his possessions, his pocketbook. If man is not willing to take his material resources along into the support of his spiritual and mental interests, he is leaving out an important element, which will undoubtedly result in his failure to achieve anything of value from the experience.

Responding at all levels is the completion of the circle of life. Without it, man and his activity are short-circuited. Those who undertake a business venture, take a vacation, or play a sport should seek to have a full, complete experience with mental, material, and spiritual rewards as well.

The reason the sport of surfing has gained such prominence in this day among the young and others is because it offers another dimension that other sports do not. In hardly any other sport is there a moving, changing, challenging natural element asking for communication. A successful ride combines communion with nature, mental skill, and physical agility in a most satisfying and complete experience.

Every activity, every experience offers man mystical fulfillment if he realizes and takes his whole self into it.

CHAPTER 3

THE MAZE AND THE MAP

The familiar story of *Alice Through the Looking Glass* explains how Alice stepped from the confines of her ordinary inanimate world through the looking glass into a world where chessmen, flowers, and the most ordinary objects took on a kind of psychedelic animation. The room she saw in the mirror was a copy of the one she was in but when she went through the barrier everything took on new life.

Like Alice, today's man has stepped through the looking glass of superstition and the supernatural into revelation and the supranatural. Instead of being trapped in a world of limitation and ignorance, he is going through the mirror which had always tricked him into the limited belief that his material reflection was the whole truth of him and that his little world was an inescapable trap. Now ordinary objects have a new life and meaning, and he has the capacity to communicate and use the materials of life as never before. By making this mystical step man is no longer bound by the material limitations he had always accepted. Now that which has happened in his dreams as supernatural becomes for him very natural, in fact, supranatural. In the past when man was not able to explain many things he labeled them supernatural or called them "old wives' tales." Today science has been able to replace superstitious beliefs with the revelation of higher supranatural truths.

Alice, before she could understand her new worlds and how to cope with them, had a problem. She had to accept the new truths she learned about old familiar objects, and she had to accept reinterpretation of the old truths. She had to adjust herself to the new discovery. We, too, have to go through a similar adjustment. For example, once we arrived at the number 144 by putting twelve twelves in a row and adding up the rows. At a later advancement we found a much more time-saving and efficient way by using cross multiplication.

Those who have not found a way to adjust, who have petrified their truths by refusing to find new and deeper understandings, huff and puff with anger because the young decline to play their way. They wonder why the young refuse to accept their rules, and they blame the young for turning away from them and their truths.

Alice found a way to adjust to a new comprehension of the old elements of her life. She met some characters who were playing cards. She saw that they were two-sided; so Alice found that in order for her to really know the meaning of the individual she was encountering she had to see both sides of the card, a total picture. This, too, is not far from today. You can take a playing card, or any object, hold it in your hand and ask yourself if you know the truth of it. The answer can only be in the negative. You can see the truth of the size of the card in relation to your hand. It is rectangular, flat, made of paper, covered with markings, and so on, but you cannot see the atoms it is made up of with your naked eye, and you certainly cannot see that the electrons are whirling around in space like universes in themselves; you cannot see any of the other aspects that science tells us about.

The solution to Alice's problem and the resolution of her story came as Alice learned how to find a whole and balanced truth about the objects and situations she was confronted with. She learned to look for and be able to contain an awareness of all sides at the same time. She learned to talk to herself and remind herself of all aspects until she could find her own balance and freedom from ignorance. In order to fully understand a truth, it becomes necessary to hold a thought in a state of suspension while other aspects are seen and a whole truth arrived at—a whole truth that transcends one-sided reason.

All human life is divided up into what Orientals call "the pairs of opposites," into truth and illusion, into spirit and matter, into right and wrong. In order to attain a higher sense of truth, however, we must come to a point when a kind of conscious "double thinking" is necessary. Double thinking is not a combination of seeing 50 per cent of one side and 50 per cent of the other, not accepting 80 per cent of one aspect and blending it with 20 per cent of the other. Rather, it is a matter of seeing a full 100 per cent of both sides at the same time—one aspect held in a state of suspension while the other is recognized, comprehended, and understood, but neither rejected.

Those who attempt to reject or condemn all the material side of life are trying to split life in two and are one-sided. On the other hand, those who believe that the material appearance is the sum and total of life are one-sided. The union of the outside and the inside, the material and spiritual, in a mystical oneness requires a conscious desire and ability for double thinking. Double thinking, this double thread, is a most important key to open the door to the mystical life.

The Purpose of Life

The hopes of man soar when he dares to believe that he can live this mystical life in actual personal contact with the source that replaces the supernatural with the supranatural. Why, then, is man floundering around in this maze called life?

The same question might be asked about why man goes to school. The answer hinges on the fact that there is a world of difference between unconscious, unrealized truth, and conscious realized truth. On many occasions we have seen those with instinctive talent perform beautifully at one time and miss at another because they did not have a conscious knowledge or control of their craft or talent. A real understanding would have made them not only more productive, but more consistent, free of hit-and-miss results.

Individuals undergo the experience of being humans as a process of evolution from unconscious living to the conscious realization of their selves, their powers, and their source. On the other hand the collective universal consciousness of mankind is expanding, and as the greater number of individuals attain a higher consciousness of truth, truth itself becomes more perfectly expressed.

Finite man has always been part of infinity, but by not having a conscious awareness of his source he has felt cut off, alone. With the awakening to the truth of self comes the elimination of the sense of desperation or aloneness. The finite is not aware of infinity, but infinity encompasses or touches all of the finite. Finite man is learning to stretch to infinity.

We might look at it this way. When an employer has reached the maximum of capacity and wishes to expand his creative capability, he must delegate authority to his employees. They only learn by trial and error and they only learn if they have the authority to make mistakes as well as to produce. Through their mistakes they acquire the consciousness of the master. Therefore, as man goes through this human experience he learns, by trial and error as much as by anything else, the conscious use of his creative faculties, and more creation results.

The human experience itself is a kind of "prodigal son" voyage. There is always the trip out and the trip back to the source. The same process takes place in every act of creativity. If a potter wants to fashion a pot, he must first rip an amount of clay from the source, the ground. Seen in its unrefined state the clay is useless, but then in its trip back it is formed into a thing of beauty.

Universally speaking, astronomers have discovered what they call Blue Quaziers, farther out in space than anything discernible before, from which they can evaluate the world's history in time. They explain that the universe itself expands outwardly and finally comes back on itself —a kind of heavenly prodigal son story. But it is our story and the story of all creativity. When we return, we return with a conscious realization of the ground of our being. That can happen only by a transformation of consciousness, an awakening to the truth of ourselves.

Where We Are and Where We Expect To Get

We start any trip knowing where we are at the moment and where we want to end. Then we choose the best map to show us how to get there. At the moment, generally speaking, man is fragmented. He was part of the whole, but as his intellect grew he became more and more fragmented, more isolated.

Every time man invented more organizations, more governments, more institutions, he broke himself off from his fellow man. Every invention he brought forth stretched him and added to the infinite variety of man. As Marshall McLuhan has said in his book *Understanding*

Media: The Extensions of Man, every invention became an extension of man. The telephone is an extension of the ear. The wheel is an extension of the foot. Television is the extension of the eye. Now man's hearing is not confined to a few feet, his eye does not stop at the horizon. He can see and hear any sight or sound made at any place on earth at any moment. This fragmentation, which really began its tremendous acceleration with the arrival of the Industrial Revolution, has been exploding man.

With the invention of modern transportation man was no longer contained in a life that allowed him to range only a few miles from his home in a day's time. With modern communications, radio, television, the press and such, man was made aware of his own potential. By seeing what other men were able to accomplish, man was torn open by his own desire not to be limited. If he had not been able to see and know many men, he would not have had such a wide range to measure himself by and he would not have expected so much of himself.

When communications showed him the infinite possibilities within himself, despite the fact that he was surrounded by more humans than ever before, he felt more cut off, more fragmented. Thereupon he became aware of a more acute loneliness than he had ever experienced. It did not help that loneliness is a part of growing up, that a child leaves the security of his parents and goes out into loneliness in order to find his own fulfillment.

Today, in place of the fragmented family life, many try to replace the family with the city. There is no place where loneliness is felt more acutely than in the city. The multiplicity of city life fragments the individual all the more.

The reason for the dissolution of the family circle—one of the most obvious changes of this present day—is the ease of transportation and communication. Originally a family stuck together for purposes of protection, communication, supply, food, and such. Now transportation is so quick and available, communications so simple, and supply so mobile that there is nothing to glue the family together.

The fragmentation of the individual, and possibly of the family, is nearing completion. The prodigal son is at the end of the road. At present the need and direction is toward a returning to wholeness of the individual and society. That is the goal of the journey.

This return to wholeness, this renewed wholeness, fulfills all the aims the seers of the ages have wanted for mankind. Some people fear that if mankind does join together in a cooperative and whole family of man, it will mean the end of individuality. But they need have no fear. What appears as a diminishing of individuality will rather be seen as a platform for a more exquisite superindividuality. Man once spent almost all of his time and energy in feeding, clothing, and sheltering his body in pursuit of personal security and protection. With the realization that the family is now all of mankind, enormous amounts of wasted time will be eliminated. Man will cooperate in using his modern inventions to take care of all human needs. New-found sources of energy will relieve man of unnecessary time and effort. Then individual man will have time to express his individuality in creative ways almost imcomprehensible to today's world.

If that is where we are going, we need some directions, some tools to work with, a map. As this human experience is a voyage, we can either flounder around on our own or find some direction from the materials at hand and from those who have made the trip.

Finding Directions

Science can be the map for many. Sages and seers of thousands of years ago spiritually discerned a number of things that are today being given scientific proof. The sages did not know why they were true; they just knew that they were true, but science has revealed the way. Ancient sages proclaimed that time was not a reality, yet the great scientific sage, Albert Einstein, came up with a mathematical equation proving that time is not real, only relative, and from his revelation man has split the atom. Scientists find that if they can discover how a principle works in one area, they can successfully apply that principle in another area. They begin to uncover eternal truths.

Another way to find direction in life is through the aesthetic approach. As great art reveals life, both the study of art itself and the lessons one learns in mastering its techniques can be applied to living creatively. By the same token, the lives of great men can be studied to give clues about how we can live. If they accomplished a lot they must have had some successful formula for living by which we can gain help. Life itself offers us many paths depending on the temperament and capacity of each of us as individuals.

In recognition that there are as many different paths as there are different types of humans, the Hindu culture set down different instructions each one could follow in accord with his individual personality. The word *yoga* just means "path," and there are many yogas. In the West we are most familiar with the purely physical system of yoga, but that is only one of the paths to freedom. Janana Yoga is the intellectual approach. Karma Yoga is the action or "do unto others as you would have them do unto you" approach. Bakti is a more devotional or ceremonial way. Those in the same family, though all Hindu, can choose separate maps to follow.

Every facet of life reflects itself in the literature of the world. As a matter of fact, literature is made up of the experiences of man and his life. Man has used literature to record his most minute movements as well as his greatest extravagances. It is natural, then, that man turns to books when he wants to find guidance and instruction.

When we shop around for textbooks or materials with which to learn and work, we naturally want to find the most practical and proven texts. For advice, we turn to the masters for they have proven by their works that they have a creative consciousness. Though writers come and go, the plays of a Shakespeare remain through the years. Fables and myths live while gossip and fiction die out. Why? A thing lives in the degree to which it expresses a depth of truth. The plays of Shakespeare reveal fundamental truths about human nature that remain because they are true, and truth does not change. The same is true about fables, myths, and even fairy tales. Behind any surviving thing there is, in mathematical ratio to its life span, truth supporting it.

If we are going to use literature, the next step is to decide what literature to use. We look around, therefore, for the writings in our culture which have remained most powerful and dominant through the years as a source of the greatest truth. Like it or not, the giant of all literary works for the Western world in its effect, place, importance, and influence through the ages has been the collection of writings we call the Holy Bible. The Bible is not the writings of one man alone, and it covers the span of many years. Therefore, it is not only full of tales of insane vindictiveness, tribal mishmash, garbled history, and raffish myth, but it is also full of the glory of wisdom, beauty, poetry, and the crowning triumph of the story of the most influential man in history, Jesus of Nazareth. Obviously the secrets of life are contained in it somehow as it has continued to live, plague, and placate man.

We could choose a lesser work than the Bible and learn a lot, but why not dare to see if we can find some sense or order where so many have assaulted its text with varying degrees of success. If we have long ago given up trying to understand it because of the indigestible interpretations that have been crammed down our throats, or if we have not tried at all because of its reputation, let's take a chance in the light of the new instruments we have of thought. If we approach it, let us do so as though it were a new book that we have never before seen. If it is already a source of inspiration, let us check our cherished beliefs and see if it isn't a great enough source to reveal new light. At least it comes closer to being a common ground of recognition than any other works we have to study.

The Bible, or scriptures, has always been difficult to use. The most notable example is that almost none of those who heard Jesus really understood him. In that respect he was a failure. The Jews, to whom he spoke, rejected his message. But the Gentiles to whom he did not personally speak, got some of his message and carried it on through the years. The reason is that Jesus used the old familiar scriptures with which all the Jews were familiar. This made it easy for the minds of the people to miss the subtle, but all-important, new meanings. Those who heard him just could not shake off the old, accepted concept; so the new could not take hold and work.

It is just as difficult today. There is a perfectly valid reason why many people, old and young, wish to reject all the scriptures, references to the Bible, and Christian jargon. Their instincts sense how easily their minds can and have distorted the subtleties of any attempted new interpretation. They would much rather start with fresh material where the mind could not have such a field day of easy distortion. But a whole person is one who can tackle this most profound source of eternal truth and confusion, comprehend that which is for him, and be free enough to leave the rest.

Scholars have pointed out before that every basic plot, every drama, takes place somewhere in the Bible. All the dramas that have come from the pen of playwrights have, in some way or another, been variations on the themes of human nature found there. Though the Bible is made up of the stories of individual people, collectively it adds up to the story of universal man. Just as the individual man develops and has developed over the years, the universal man, or universal consciousness, has also reached a point in its collective development. Individual man went through the whole agony of the Old Testament experience until that day when something was born in individual man which we call the Christ, which then grew into its fullness and freedom. If this is the beginning of the spiritual day, or the day when the universal man accepts the mystical approach to life, then this is the day when perhaps the birth of the Christ has taken place in the universal man.

If the New Testament illustrates the stages of development of the individual into fullness, then perhaps it can give some direction to the fulfillment of universal consciousness. It is said that man is a microcosm in a macrocosm, a complete little world operating inside a big world with all the same rules and problems. The principles that apply to the individual are the same as those for the body of mankind and the universe.

CHAPTER 4

THE OLD AND
THE NEW

In the most general terms, the Old Testament represents the first half of the prodigal trip away from home or wholeness. It is, from the first, a progression of confusion, disorder, and fragmentation. That is one of the reasons why the Old Testament is so much harder to read than the New. It is not only full of so many "begats" that one would need a most elaborate diagram of the cast of characters to follow it, but it also contains all the confusion that we wish to untangle in our own lives. Just about the time the reader begins to see a pattern and begins to think, "Ah, now I will find some rules to follow or some practical suggestions I can apply to life," the story takes a turn where for some mysterious reason the hero mercilessly punishes his neighbor, goes to war, and lays whole cities flat, and, what's more, with the help of God. A literal interpretation leads to seemingly hopeless confusion.

The New Testament represents the prodigal's return to

wholeness and order. All of humanity is summed up and given an example in the life of one man. The pieces of the Old are there taken and put in their right order to form a whole and show a direction that all can profit from and follow.

The prodigal trip is the creative principle behind any act of creating, whether it is the creation of a man or a painting. Every artist is well aware that during the process of creating a painting, the picture is in a constant state of flux, of being in balance and out of balance. Finally, right at the end, the final dot of color goes into place, the picture is in balance—and it is finished. Though it is now dead to its old way of life, it assumes a new kind of life. It is hung on the wall and, though no longer in motion, no longer being created, it becomes an inspiration and a joy to others. It even becomes a map to help them create.

The Bible illustrates that we, like the picture on the artist's easel, are going through this creative process. We are constantly in and out of balance during our whole lifetime. We are up one minute and down the next—like someone on a seesaw. At first we ride the seesaw helplessly plunging from harmony into discord, from fear to joy, and back again. We clutch at anything, any law, that might give us something to hang on to, but because we are drunk with confusion we do as much harm as good. This drunken state might be called our Old Testament confusion. When we are operating without guidance or direction, we can say we are under the disorder of the old.

Finally something like the birth of truth, the birth of the Christ consciousness, takes place within us. We begin to see the purpose of our experience, what our potential is, and the possibility of getting in rhythm with life. We are not out of the woods just because this birth has taken place, but now we are shown the possibility of freedom.

We are given instructions to follow and an example. When we begin to know who we are, we begin to sober up. As the dizziness abates we stop fighting the seesaw and start getting in rhythm with life. We start slowly. First we tap a finger, then a hand, than a foot, until finally we learn to dance with our whole being. Great teachers, such as the master of them all, Jesus, are like great conductors who point out the rhythms of life. Out of the discord of the Old Testament came the symphonic harmony of the New.

The confusion in being able to understand the basic difference between the Old and New has led men to think the two could be used interchangeably. Almost all of the elements of the New can be found somewhere in the Old, and there are signs of confusion in the New as well as in the Old because the New does not sort out the confusion and draw its conclusions until its fulfillment. The differences are subtle, and when one snatches bits from the Old and interjects them in the New it can only compound the confusion and cause the New to be obscured. For this reason there are few purely Christian churches. Most churches operate partly under the edicts and laws of the Old and partly under the message of Grace which is unique to the New.

It is commonly accepted that the Old Testament is symbolized by man's attempt to live by law, which is based on judgment. The unique difference of the New Testament way of life is that it instructs man to live by something called Grace, which is based on "righteous" judgment. Man had failed to succeed in his attempt to live by human judgment and law; so the New Testament showed him a way he could succeed in fulfilling the law if he lived by Grace based on righteous judgment. The key is in understanding the meaning of judgment.

Legally a judgment is the decision of the cause. The court bases its decision on its finding of what caused the condition it is examining. As imagination is the cause, any situation is the result of some idea or thought someone had to begin with; judgment is another name for the action of imagination. When we judge we are imagining. Therefore our lives are created out of our judgments.

Of the two kinds of judgment there is human judgment and there is righteous or spiritual judgment. The human is judging from the outside in and the spiritual is judging from the inside out. Whenever the judgment is based on appearances, on the limitations of matter and the phenomenal world, it is human judgment, and whenever it is based on the mystical identification with the source or the invisibles, it is spiritual judgment. This applies to you and me in this way. Whenever we believe that we are cut off from the source of life, that our security is based on things, our money, our health, our guns, we are judging with our human sense. We do not judge a small scratch because we feel there is little harm in it, but if it becomes infected and we believe it has the power to kill us, we start judging in ratio to our fear of it.

If we find some money, get a new job or a stronger body, we judge that as good. The whole Old Testament experience happened when Eve ate of the fruit of the tree of good and evil and created human judgment, which was based on good and bad. Both are human judgments.

Human judgment believes that there is cause in effect. It believes that inanimate created things have power, forgetting that all things were created out of imagination or consciousness. Instead of changing the imagination in order to change the form, whenever we fight the form we are judging it as bad and we only create more of it.

It is said that the first law of human nature is the law of self-preservation. Human nature thus judges anything that will help one survive as good and anything that lessens one's well-being as bad. Living by this law, a person fights whatever he believes is bad and thereby creates more of the same thing. He goes deeper and deeper into bondage.

In order to put this law into perspective and become free of its effect on our own lives we need to understand it in terms of some double thinking. As we have said, man is not one-sided while on earth. There are times when he is operating mainly under the first law of human nature, and there are times when he is operating under the righteous judgment where he does not judge by appearances. If one wants to figure out how the human side is going to react, one should apply the first law of human nature. A man's human nature will always make for him the decision that he feels will increase his security, make him safer, wealthier, and happier. Human nature feels cut off, and his decision will not be based on what is good for another person. The mistake we make is when we try to believe that mankind will act otherwise, out of love. So if one is operating purely in the crass human world he had better make his decisions based on that law.

But that is only half the picture. Most of us are on the seesaw, but most of us have had something like the birth of the Christ within us. Most of us have times when we are not operating purely under the law of human nature. We believe that the invisibles are more important than the visibles. We realize that the ends do not justify the means. We sense that there is an invisible source behind life that is more important than our human security, and at those times we are operating under what might be called the first law of spiritual nature. When man realizes that he is not dealing with person, place, condition, or thing in the external and that he must go within his own self and there resolve the appearance into a whole truth, he is living under the first law of spiritual nature. In other words, when man does not believe that there is cause in effect, he is approaching the mystical way of living. This is what the New Testament meant by righteous judgment.

When he follows the instruction, "Take no thought for the morrow, what ye shall eat, or what ye shall wear," he is judging righteously. When he follows the New Testament instruction, "Know ye no man after the flesh," he is judging righteously.

There is a world of difference between judgment and a statement of fact, and one needs double thinking to keep from confusing them. A statement of fact is unconditioned by a sense of good and evil. One can say, "She is seven feet tall," or "He is black," and there is no judgment. But if one says, "She's a freak," or "He's a nigger," it is human judgment and has the power of evil imagination behind it.

The basis of the uprisings on the campuses of America and the most dominant single theme in the rebellious cry of the young is their desire to be free of the human judgments on which so much of our way of life has been based. Older people think that the students are rebelling over which is better: communism or democracy, peace or war, right or wrong. In a sense that is true, but behind it is the paramount desire to live a life based on spiritual judgment or, rather, lack of human judgment. The students are saying, "It isn't a matter of right and wrong. There is no justification, one way or the other, in using force to achieve one's goal. There is no justification ever for war, harm, lack of love, or judgment based on selfish desires."

Law Or Grace

Human judgment gave rise to human law. Man's human judgment created such confusion and fragmentation that he had to find some system to live by. He thought that if he could find what was the greatest good for the greatest number he could have a yardstick to live by. He tried to find such a law for every human situation, but this had a major fault and limitation. Not only was it impossible to encompass enough laws for the infinity of the human experience, but law became one-sided. In light of the illustration we used earlier, a minus is a minus but there is a time, not often but occasionally, when two minuses make a plus. The fault of law is that when the time comes where someone is right in saying that a minus is a plus, it has no way of taking this into account. The individual must be sacrificed to the fact that most of the time a minus is a minus. He becomes the victim of law, innocent or not.

Because man did not realize that he had that within him that would tell him what was correct for each situation, he formed institutions to formulate systems of law. These institutions became crutches for men to lean on to tell them how to live. The institutions further separated man from man. Governments and nations became systems of law, and man was divided from other men because some followed one system and others another. When man abdicated his individual right to sense what was right, he placed himself in human bondage to finite organization and cut himself off from the source of life itself. The significance of this abdication of personal freedom is that, bit by bit, as man placed his life in the hands of law, he made a kind of god out of law.

When law became a kind of god, the human mind became a kind of god to man. Man, not having faith or belief in himself, began to let his mind live his life instead of being a balanced person where body, mind, and spirit joined together as his life. His mind said what was bad or good, what was law or violation of law. His mind said, "Don't trust your inner feelings. Don't believe you have the capacity to know what the loving or spiritual thing to do is. Don't believe that you can sense the time when the opposite of the common truth is true for you. You are not worthy of freedom. You must always make sense and be logical. You do not have that within you which will maintain and sustain you. I will live your life for you and tell you what you should do and what you should not." But what else could man do? He was hypnotized by false judgment and by the misguided imagination that created his chaos. It placed him under the bondage of law and his mind. Then the New Testament message of Grace and righteous judgment showed him a way to freedom.

Righteous judgment places a great responsibility on the individual and leaves him nowhere to hide. That is why the weak like to hide behind organization. As humans we want "off the hook." We search around for places to put the blame. But the law of righteous judgment is that we realize that whatever appears in our life is the product of our own imagination, our own consciousness. It tells us that we must never fight the thing or condition that is on the outside but must go within and there correct the cause. It is easy to be tempted on the outside to judge that another person is the cause of our trouble, that a government limits our supply by taxing us, or even that a piece of food has brought on our sickness, for man has lived humanly under these laws through most of his life. But righteous judgment does not let us take that easy way out.

To go within for guidance is to be "in the world, but not of it." The kingdom of heaven is within because the power to attain the consciousness of righteous judgment is within. When we learn that the kingdom of heaven is within we find that within is the possibility of freedom. No matter how many times the master revealed that the kingdom of heaven was actually and positively within, man has placed it outside, has prayed to it, lit candles to it, and begged of it. Freedom certainly is a kind of inner heaven. That possibility is within the consciousness of each individual, is within each individual on earth. By the same token, "My kingdom is not of this world" is to say "My kingdom, protection, joy, and freedom are realized as not being in things as cause, not being at the level of externals; but rather, my freedom is in knowing the source, and the source manifests itself in all I want."

So often it has mistakenly been believed that Jesus meant that his kingdom was off in the clouds, apart from this earth. Were that the case, he would never have been on earth. He was actually saying that the kingdom of heaven is right here, right now. "The ground on which ye stand is holy ground," if you could but open your eyes and see. "Ye have eyes and ye see not; ye have ears and ye hear not," because you are using eyes as material instruments testifying only to the externals; using ears only to hear words instead of the spirit behind the words. No matter where you are, no matter what you are doing, the truth is present, awaiting your recognition; so there is nothing occult or supernatural in saying that the kingdom, the Christ, the truth, consciousness are present where you are.

Man puts on truth, puts on immortality as mortality disappears. When he has the capacity to see beyond appearances to the consciousness, he is no longer bound by human concepts and he can say, as did the Master, "I have overcome the world." I have overcome the limitation of seeing this earth through the eyes of ignorance. Then, and only then, can we say we are living by Grace.

The Meaning of Grace

The word Grace is so overloaded with different meanings that it needs reexamination. In worldly terms it is used for anything from describing a beauty of form or manner to the address of royalty. Theologically many believe that Grace is some kind of special dispensation for those who are in favor, a virtue of divine origin. Grace is actually the perfect, pure, eternal, and impersonal principle of life and creativity. Grace is truth in action.

Things and people exist. Something, some kind of intelligence, some law of creativity brought everything into being. There is a ground for all this being. There is some kind of activity of truth that forms this intricate body. The mother was used as the instrument, but an intelligence at present beyond man's comprehension formed this complicated machine called man. There is some truth that makes orange seeds grow into orange trees and produce more oranges. There is something that makes the tides come in and go out with regularity, and sustains this earth in the heavens. Whatever this creative principle of the universe is, whatever maintains and sustains life, whatever heals a sickness or mends a bone we can call the activity of Grace.

Grace is the source of life; so, like the alphabet, it is for our use, but it cannot be hoarded, it cannot be used up or worn out. When we individualize it with a degree of truth and beauty we can become great poets or Shakespeares. But Grace is impersonal. So it does no good to pray to it or beg of it any more than it does good to pray to the alphabet to make poetry. Like the sun, it is always there for all; everything gets its life from it, but the fact that it exists is not enough. We must go out into it. We must not block it by human judgment, but we must come in line with its creative powers by righteous judgment. If we keep the blinds of ignorance pulled over our intelligence or judgments, it will do us no good. We must go out and experience the sun, truth, or Grace.

On the other hand, Grace is like an umbrella. It is there for our protection as long as we stay beneath its shelter. It isn't the fault of the umbrella if we, out of ignorance and self-will, do not make use of it. The umbrella does not comprehend us at the level of our personal ignorance nor tell us how to use it properly. We must learn to listen to the still small voice within ourselves that signals when we are judging humanly, when a truth is not a whole truth. Then we can get reestablished with fulfilling creation.

The great and wonderful thing about Grace is that it not only continues to operate despite our attempts to frustrate it, but, like the water of a stream when it has been dammed, it fills up behind our obstacles and eventually flows forth again. We can say that two times two are five and get the wrong answer over and over, but finally we are driven to finding that two times two are four and we are reestablished in creative harmony. Mathematics, like Grace, does not punish us, but the fact that it is the truth of being leads us to a conscious awareness of its principles and help.

Whereas the laws of man relate to the world of finite objects, the phenomenal world, Grace relates to the invisible source of all being. Grace then manifests itself at the finite level in fulfillment for the whole law in the finite terms of greater harmony, greater supply, and greater peace. The paradox is that when one turns his eyes from the material world and attains a sense of righteous judgment, material limitations fall away, and the rewards one desired as a human now come about. There is no accident in this, nothing supernatural. It does not even require an act of faith to realize that Grace is operating behind our daily lives. When one has water and 212 degrees of temperature one has boiling water. It is not accidental.

Those who are searching to find freedom from the bondage of the material sense of value are approaching the mystical life where one lives by the Grace of truth. Jesus was a man who lived totally by Grace. The individual who has accepted this, or who is attempting to live by Grace and righteous judgment, is experiencing the second coming of Christ—first as another man named Jesus and second within himself.

CHAPTER 5

THE SEARCH AND THE SECRET

Once upon a time, as all fairy tales begin, there was a halo around the word "security." Security was the reward at the end of the rainbow, and all good little boys and girls had but one thought, to achieve security. As most of the world is still living under the spell of that illusion, most people are still seeking something they think they want but actually do not.

Man's first desire is to be alive, to live, to express life. But the mind of man, acting as the wicked wizard, has hypnotized man into thinking that security is life when, in fact, it is death. If you take a seed and put it in an airtight bottle on the shelf, it will appear secure for a thousand years, like the sleeping prince, but indeed, it is dead, inactive, unfulfilled. A seed must fall into the ground, die, and break open for a tree to grow from it, for it to be alive.

We judge how alive a person or situation is according to the amount of creativity that is taking place. We say,

"Boy, that company is really alive. Look how they are expanding, how much more they are producing." Yet no creativity takes place when there is a total security because a secure thing is immovable and unchangeable. I cannot leave this piece of wood secure and carve a statue out of it at the same time. I cannot leave the eggs in their shells and bake a cake with them. There must be an element of insecurity in order to create, to be what we call alive.

It is the natural desire and instinct to live and be creative that makes the young wish to break out of the security of their family background. Like school, the family relationship is based considerably on the laws of human life and cooperation. Like school, family relationship represents a time when the young become familiar with the tools of life and develop their mental and physical muscles. But there comes a time when the need for insecurity in order to be individually creative pushes within the young adult, and he feels hemmed in by law. He begins to become aware of the wisdom of insecurity and the necessity of it in order to exert his God-given right to be creative and alive.

Security is a crutch man leans on to avoid having to depend on that which he has within himself to be creative. Indeed, as long as he leans on a crutch he is inactive and uncreative.

Crutches

As human beings we lean on many crutches. We believe that our security lies in the money we have in the bank, and we lean on that; we believe that our companionship comes from our family, and we lean on that; we believe that our health comes from good habits of diet, and we lean on that. Ultimately we believe that there are ideas and theologies we can understand with our minds, and we lean on them as crutches. But these are crutches and until we realize the wisdom of human insecurity and start to place our complete reliance on a life lived by Grace, we suffer as the crutches are knocked out from under us.

The master said that "foxes have holes, and the birds of the air have nests, but the Son of Man hath nowhere to lay his head." To be the son of man, to have that state of consciousness that was in Christ Jesus, is to live without external crutches and to place all reliance on the truth of being, on a life lived by inner Grace.

We only have to take a good look at our lives to see in how many places we place our trust. Even if we have a teaching or theology that is so real to us that we believe it has all the answers and can be our crutch, we are in danger of laying our head on that. Jesus said, "If I go not away, the comforter will not come unto you," for otherwise his disciples would have continued more and more to lean on him as a man and not find their own fulfillment, their own sonship with the source of being. Any time a teacher sits down and allows students to come to him, study with him, start to deify him, and eventually lean on him he is not operating under pure truth or spirit.

The thermometer of life swings up and down in relation to the degree to which one's crutches are being threatened. One need not speculate on the degree of another's sense of faith or security, for it is by another's reactions to his experiences that the true degree of inner security is revealed. If you go tell one man that his house is on fire and he panics, you know that to that degree he believes his good is wrapped up in a material house. If you go to another one and tell him that his house is on fire and he says, "Well now, let's go splash some water on it," you know that that man is secure within, that he does not believe his good is in a thing but rather in his ability to create another if that is destroyed.

Today there is rising alarm at the increase in the num-

ber of people who have to go to the hospitals for emotional disturbances. Most of those are people who have
not been able to cope with life when their crutches were
removed. In place of the crutches they have been given
tranquilizers. But tranquilizers are only temporary helps.
Only when they learn to lean on something within themselves will they be able to adjust to this fast-changing
world.

One's ability to cope with this coming day will be in
direct ratio to one's ability to survive without leaning on
the crutches of today, and to one's ability to place reliance
in a security based on something other than the world of
effect. How can this be done?

The Revelation

Jesus, as the master guide, revealed to us a secret that has
either been lost to mankind or been overlooked. Perhaps
this one secret is the unique difference between his teaching and that of all the others. The aspiration of all the
world's religions, or the goal of all the various systems of
religious thought, has been to achieve oneness, to eliminate duality, to be in harmony with the rhythm of the
universe. Each in turn has failed because its followers did
not realize the necessity of the instruction Jesus gave to
his followers or else they overlooked the importance of this
key, as most so-called Christians have. In the admirable
attempt to eliminate duality almost everyone has divided
the world up into spiritual and material, into reality as
opposed to illusion, and by doing so has actually created
the very duality he wished to eliminate.

Jesus' answer, perhaps his secret, was revealed in his
own words. When the men of that day, who were trying
to find solution to the problems of living by comprehending the many laws, came to Jesus for guidance, they asked
him instruction in law. They asked him about the Ten

Commandments. He replied, "Take the first [implying they should not be concerned with the other nine] and add to it a second which is like unto the first." The first Commandment was the instruction to love God, and he added to it a second which was the instruction to love man. God represented the invisible, infinite, and humanly unidentifiable aspect of life, and the neighbor represented all we could see and recognize in finite form, whether man or object. The secret was the fact that it was necessary to accept an apparent duality in order to achieve a true oneness.

As the instruction was to know the true nature of the visible and the invisible, of the spiritual and the natural, so the moment man turned his collar around and withdrew from the world into a monastic mountaintop, he turned his back on the world, and he was doomed to fail in his goal to achieve oneness. The moment man decided he could find all the answers at the level of test tube and action, he too missed the way to freedom, this double thread.

Most of the Oriental religions spent their search in the vertical relationship of man to invisible God. They ignored the lateral necessity of knowing and identifying with their fellow man. By saying that the world was "maya" or illusion, they were denying that there was any reality to materiality. They were actually sitting in condemnation of the material scene by trying to blot it out. They were not judging righteously. To know the world of God, we must know the truth of the world of matter; not reject it, run from it, or hide from it, but know it.

Today, under the title of absolute teachings, there are those who mistakenly believe that all one must do is to know God. These teachings do little to bring harmony in the lives of those who believe that such a one-sided approach to life is the answer; their material problems of health and supply are not solved. If all that were needed was to know God, we would not have been given the two commandments. It is stated that "the greater of these is the love of God." Nevertheless we were given the lesser as a necessary adjunct.

Many in the metaphysical fields have rightly been in awe of their discovery that the power of the invisible can so visibly affect their lives only to lose the double thread. They get so involved in learning and using invisible truths of spirit that they start to ignore the world of human existence. They begin to get cold and impersonal about other people's needs, forgetting that the master said, "Inasmuch as ye have done it unto one of the least of these my brethren, ye have done it unto me," or if someone asks for bread, don't give him a stone. Don't give him a cold impersonal truth.

The Buddhists came close to the knowledge of the need of this double thread in their interpretation of the Yin and Yang of life, but though they thereby accepted the material existence, many then relegated the material to the area of unimportance and missed the need to see each side equally in order to find union of self and life. When giving us this secret, the Master was actually advocating a kind of double thinking. It is impossible consciously to know and think about the finite and to be aware of infinity at the same precise moment. But it is possible to look at the finite aspect and hold it in mind while the infinite is comprehended and a balance arrived at. In other words, things do not have to be "either, or." We do not have to think that if one thing is true another cannot be.

The story of Martha and Mary illustrates this to some extent. Mary sat at the feet of the Master, ignoring the practical responsibilities of the material side of life but drinking in the commandment of the love of the invisible truth and spirit. Martha represented the human needs and labored as hard in her way to fulfill them. The Master admitted, as he did when he gave us the two commandments, that the love of pure infinite truth and spirit was perhaps the better part—because being infinite it included all—but he also gave full credit to the other side, the material side. He knew that the Martha side was as necessary as the Mary side.

Freedom and oneness are achieved when the two aspects are brought into balance. This balance we must each discover for ourselves. The desire to find a formula for balance that would fit everyone is what led man to law. But as man has infinite individuality perfect balance can only be found by Grace. No one can reach within another's inner listening nor hear another's still small voice. No one can tell just how much weight to put on one side of another's scale so that he will be perfectly balanced. To live by Grace is to be able to turn within at any moment and find out if, how, and where you are out of balance.

How to Walk the Razor's Edge

The aim of man has long been to find this perfect state of balance, to walk the razor's edge. He has gone to incredible lengths in attempting this and has always failed. Man would no longer be on earth if he could really stand on the razor's edge. Like the seesaw ride, when he achieves perfect balance he gets off the seesaw. Nevertheless, something equivalent to walking the razor's edge can be performed by man.

Man can work in the world, be occupied with the activity of human existence or law and, at the same time, if he is living by Grace, he can sense when he is too much out of balance, too far away from seeing the world through his spiritual eyes. When he realizes this, he can pull himself up and cross over to the other side, spend more time releasing his limited view, stop thinking in terms of material values, and can contemplate the absolute or unconditioned state of being. After a time the same inner direction of Grace can warn him that he is losing touch with the world of men, that he has human responsibilities too, and he can once again cross over, balancing his spiritual activity with human activity. The result is that he can end up with a life that averages the two sides. The average is the razor's edge.

Jesus averaged the razor's edge. When he had worked too long in the market, when he had healed and taught, and been concerned for the world to the limit of his balance, he would then retire to the mountaintop. There he would be alone with God, with absolute truth and the source of all his strength and power. There were still people needing to be healed and taught, but that was of no concern to him until he got himself restored and in balance. Then once more he would return to the world of men. He was a balanced man in tune with every side of life.

Reconciliation

This ability to gain balance was the ability to reconcile the visible and the invisible. The Bible itself calls this message "the ministry of reconciliation" and "the word of reconciliation." In fact, these verses from the fifth chapter of Second Corinthians state it clearly: "If any man be in Christ [if any man attain the same state of consciousness], he is a new creature: old things are passed away [old one-sided vision]; behold all things become new [now that they are seen wholly]. And all things are of God [the infinite], who hath reconciled us to himself by Jesus Christ [finite man], and hath given to us the ministry of reconciliation; to wit, that God [truth] was in Christ, reconciling the world unto himself [reconciling the visible and the invisible], not imputing their trespasses unto them [not seeing them in terms of their limitations alone]; and hath committed unto us the word of reconciliation."

Now we see that this path we are taking is the path of reconciliation, reconciling the world with the truth of being. The passage states that this consciousness was not sent to impute the faults and weaknesses of man's judgment to the world, rather, that by knowing the "word of reconciliation" the world might be freed, freed from ignorance. The two commandments—the love of God and the love of man—are the tools Jesus has given us to work with. He claims that we only need these two and that with them we can fulfill all of what man wanted under law, we can achieve a perfect state of Grace. We use the two tools to reconcile life into one stream, into one double thread.

CHAPTER 6

TO LOVE ANOTHER

Before attempting to intercept what Jesus meant by the commandment to love our neighbor and how to do it, it is necessary to find a disinfected or uncluttered meaning for the word "love." Love is the key word in deciphering the unique meaning behind the message of the whole of the New Testament as well. When this key is revealed, the New Testament can take on new meaning, be much more easily followed, and be tied together in a unity not realized before.

The performers in the stories of the Old Testament were about as confused in their understanding of what it means to love as most of us are today. There are examples where they performed every kind of human indulgence under the belief that they were loving. They were confused about the meaning because they tried to find special laws of love that could be judged and applied to each individual person or situation. Under Grace there is just one rule that fits everything. In order to find what that is, it is necessary first to strip off some of the false labels glued to the word and then see it in a pure light.

Ever since Eve desired the fruit in the Garden of Eden, man has confused love with desire. Whatever man desires he thinks he loves. That covers everything from popcorn to paper clips, from magazines to movie stars. We often hear people say, "I'd just love a dish of ice cream," or even "I loved getting that Christmas bonus." All these desires are based on human judgment of bad and good. As the first law of human nature is self-preservation, man thinks he loves anything that will make him richer, stronger, more secure, or will make him feel more free by giving him a good time. He thinks he hates anything that threatens his security. In other words his sense of love is based on appearances and false judgment.

Man feels an emotion caused by his desires. He even thinks that this emotion is love. The degree of the feeling is in line with the degree of importance the desired object has within his feeling of security. At the thought of losing the person or thing he thinks he needs, a pang of fear rises up within him. He calls the fear love. Naturally, the feeling is not always a negative one. When man achieves what he feels will make him more secure and fulfills his heart's desire, he feels excitement and exaltation. Both of these types of feeling that he mistakes for love are based in human emotion.

When man loves his own family to the exclusion of the family of mankind the same thing applies. The initial purpose of the family unit was to provide protection and security. The family was a primary need and the primary human emotion was family love. Man talked tearfully about being of the same blood, as though a microscope could tell the difference. What he really meant was that there was a common unit of security among those of the same clan where, by working together, they could protect themselves against other clans. Even today, when man stops fearing the rest of the family of mankind, he will stop feeling the emotion of hate and be able to love all men.

Jesus cleared up this false judgment about family love in the New Testament. Someone came and informed Jesus that his mother and brothers were waiting outside. To set those he was teaching straight, he clarified his own feelings. He showed he did not love his mother and brothers just because of some special biological accident that made them part of his family. He loved them because of what they were as individual people. He said, "Who is my mother? and who are my brethren?" "Whosoever shall do the will of my Father [truth] which is in heaven [purity], the same is my brother, and sister, and mother." He showed many times that he loved his family, but it was not based on the belief that they were superior to others, that they were necessary for his security; nor was it a human emotion based on desire.

Now as desire is the fuel that stimulates and colors imagination, and as imagination then creates the forms of our life, we only have to look at the forms to know if healthy or harmonious love is there. One can talk his head off about how much he loves another, but if there is constant disharmony, friction, lack of giving, discord after discord, then the consciousness of true love is not present. The people who go through all kinds of emotional and physical upheavals thinking it is love are only kidding themselves. They are indeed going through a relationship and feeling various emotions, but the experience is based on human judgment and the first law of human nature.

In order to straighten out the confusion about love it is necessary to look at the impersonal principle of love, but that seems to reduce love to a cold and intellectual chess game. It does not have to. When one sees the end result of the proper expression of love, one experiences the very warm and beatifying feeling that love can be.

The individual has an instinctive desire to be creative, to express infinity. Most often when men and women are attracted to each other it is because they recognize qualities in the other that would complete their own being, make them whole. A big tough man is attracted to a dainty delicate woman and together they make a balanced whole. The lover's desire to attain the fullness of infinity expresses itself in a personal feeling of love. This feeling and the actions of affection and sexual attraction that follow are the fruits of love. They are not the actual love, they are the results.

The sexual experience, seen as a result and not as a cause, is the high point of man's personal feeling of love. It can be man's most creative experience. Each person realizes he is not complete within himself, as a human, and to be creative the two just join in union. The primary human result is in the creation of a child, but this union can also result in creating more of a whole person for each of the people experiencing it. The man may find himself more wholly man, or the woman may find herself more wholly woman. When it is the outgrowth of true spiritual love and not a distortion of the purpose based on animal lust, it can result in a moment when the very act trancends the feeling of material limitation. This transcendence of the purely material concept of man can reveal the cornerstone of the true meaning of the word love.

True love is the ability to judge with righteous judgment. More simply, true love is the capacity to see through mere appearances to the whole person within. For example, people say, "Love is blind." They say, "John loves Mary, but everyone knows Mary is mean, weak, catty. John is so in love with her he doesn't see it." But the person who says that does not know what love is. The man who is "in love" comes closer to it. He loves Mary despite her faults or her apparent limitations. He sees her potential as being one with the source of life. He does not have to close his eyes to the faults of the one he loves. In order to love he just has to have the capacity and desire to see the truth and not judge with human judgment.

Mother Love

Mother love is the most commonly recognizable form of love. Most people think of mother love in terms of the pampering, patient, concerned catering a mother does for her family. They think that a mother raises her family by seeing that they are fed, clothed, rested, and protected; they think that the mother doctors the ills, and comforts the fears. It is indeed the mother's love that sustains and protects the family, but not as much by human ministrations as by her power of true love. By misunderstanding this power of love, by being unable to shut it off when the time has come to release the family, or by a lack of understanding of what love is, an equal amount of destruction can be brought about by the mother.

The true power of love in the mother is in the fact that she has the power to see a truth beyond the appearances. There is only one life force, and she has experienced that at the birth of her child. Every child has the potential of the Christ within him, and mother, consciously or unconsciously, realizes that. From there on in, a child may misbehave and need discipline but nevertheless, the mother knows the child was only frightened or confused and she refuses to sit in human judgment. Let a mother's son be in the death cell of the penitentiary and her lament will be, "He's a good boy—he only got in with the wrong people," because the mother's sense of the truth wants to fight through the ignorance that has hypnotized her son, the ignorance that has hypnotized him into losing his own sense of true identity. It is this power to sense the truth, this closeness with life, that pushes away the clouds of harm and ignorance and is the truth of how a mother cures and protects her family.

Because of woman's power to break through appearances to the truth of being, she has the ability to offer to the world the all-important consciousness of love, but this ability makes it harder for her to attain her own freedom. A mother has the power to look at the material scene and not judge it, but at the same time a mother's activity in life is to take care of the material needs of those around her. This necessitates a profound awareness of the material and the temptation to judge it. Unless she is well anchored in inner freedom, the slightest fear can turn the virtue of love into a weapon of bondage.

The mother's power to love is the power not to judge by the limited concepts of man under law. The amazing thing is that as long as she does not violate a sense of true love she does not break any laws! Only by knowing what love is can she fulfill the law. The ability to love is the ability not to judge man by appearance and the ability to see him free of finite limitations. This quality is easily recognizable in the saints of the past, or in those around you in the present whom you feel love you, forgive your finiteness, see you in your potential capacity.

It is impossible to love spiritually without some type of double think. In time, in man's world of human mind, there are only finite forms, limitations, flaws; but love does not exist at this level, for love is the ability to sense a truth beyond this limitation.

The Healing Love

Everyone wants mother around when he is sick because he feels there is something healing in her love as well as her attention. Everyone knows the physical pressure and heaviness he feels when he is around those who judge him harshly or expect him to make mistakes.

There are some so-called spiritual leaders who warm you with their personal concern, who make you feel a strong passion of affection in their care for your physical and spiritual well-being. Yet, though you revel in emo-

tional joy, you have few benefits from the relationship
which make your life more harmonious on the human
plane. There are other truly spiritual teachers or healers
who, though not lacking in human compassion, seem less
personally concerned with your human well-being and
from their refusal to judge by appearances you go away
healed and restored. You just have to ask yourself which
of these two kinds of love you would like to have when
you are in trouble, or need help. The person who can love
heals, whether teacher, healer, mother, or friend; he does
so purely and simply by his capacity not to judge by limited finite appearances.

The fifth chapter of Second Corinthians informed us
that we reconcile the visible and the invisible if we "know
. . . no man after the flesh." Man creates things and creates
healthy bodies in the same way—by his power to realize
the invisible potential. It then manifests itself in the visible. No amount of candle lighting, memorized prayer, or
petitioning can evoke the mystery. The experiencing of
love can. The refusal to judge by appearances is the scientific principle behind the gift of healing.

Through the centuries man has stumbled on this principle without knowing exactly what he was doing, and it
has often performed for him. Whenever there is an out-
ward demonstration of creativity or harmony, it would
not exist if the right consciousness were not somehow
perpetrating the condition. If man, with blind faith and
sheer desperation, reaches the place where he gives up
judging, releases his fearful beliefs, a healing can then
take place without his really realizing what has made it
happen. But he is ignorant of the principle and may not
be able to repeat the experience. If he knows what love
really is, he has an instrument to work with.

On the other hand, when man does not know what he is
doing he often does the opposite of that which he wants
to do. There are prayer groups of good, well-intentioned

people who meet in the worthy desire to heal those who need help, but without knowing it, they do exactly the reverse. When they bring the name of the person before the group and project that person's problem in detail and concern, they place the limited finite concept of that person in the minds of all those present. The imagination of the group is stimulated to envisage that person in a negative manner, and unless the group is strongly grounded in the capacity not to judge by appearances they add to the bondage rather than removing it.

In order, on the other hand, not to lose a total picture of the subject of healing, not to lose the double thread, it must be remembered that healing too is not "either, or." The material approach to healing through the developments of medical science has its importance in the total picture. When one has the consciousness of the commandment of the love of neighbor to the extent Jesus did when he said to the man at the well, "What's to hinder you? Take up your bed and walk," that is fine. But if man does not have that consciousness and also refuses to use the life-giving abilities of the physicians, he is being dangerously tricked by pride or ego. Again, if someone asks for bread, don't give him a stone. It is admirable to try to break the human bondage by invisible or spiritual means, and if one succeeds it proves man's transcendence over limitation. But there is no love for neighbor in withholding the aid of medical science, also God-given.

Common acceptance fosters another mistake that violates the principle of the love of neighbor—the accepted virtue of human sympathy. We have been told that it is loving to visit the sick and be sympathetic, but sympathy, as most often expressed, is a crushing handicap to the ill. Sympathy often says, "You poor thing. You are sick, aren't you? You are separate and apart from your Good. God has done this to you." And this form of judgment is exactly that from which the patient needs to be free in order to lift his consciousness back into the ease of life from the dis-ease. This is not to say that we should not visit the sick and offer them our support and compassion. If we can visit them without judging, without giving strength to ignorance, without dragging our own selves down in spirit, we can hasten freedom and are giving true love. We do not close our eyes to the condition, but we close our eyes to judgment. We know this is an appearance, and we close our eyes to labeling it bad or good in the realization that beyond law there is a reality that can and will express itself visibly.

When the New Testament is read with the true meaning of love in mind, every time the word love appears one can transpose and see it in terms of the refusal to judge by appearances. Then the true message and scope of Christian revelation is encompassed.

Not only by actual demonstration in his own life, surviving the appearance of physical destruction, but all through his teaching Jesus told us what the meaning of this love of man was. As when he said to Peter, "Who do you say I am?" Peter answered, "Thou art the Christ," (consciousness not body alone); and Jesus responded, "Ah, man did not tell you that," signifying that it was Peter's ability to love, not to judge by appearance, that was evident in that statement. "Judge not," "Know ye no man after the flesh," "Love one another"—this is how we follow the commandment of the love of neighbor.

CHAPTER 7

THE GREATEST COMMANDMENT

Jesus said that we should love our neighbor, and that we should love God. He said both are necessary, but he went on to say that the love of God is the greater of the two commandments. Anyone who has ever tried to wrestle with the meaning of the word God, to understand it, or to know what God is could only be in agreement.

It is certainly harder to know God than to know one's neighbor. We can see and listen to our neighbor. If we are broad-minded enough we can observe several characteristics of our neighbor at once and arrive at some kind of truth about him even in the face of distracting appearances. But how can we do the same for an invisible, infinite, impersonal ground or cause of all being? How can we "feel" about an abstact? It is boring and dry to even talk about abstracts. We are human beings and need human things with which to identify in order to feel. Often, when we are told we must "feel" something for and about an impersonal abstraction called God, we are really stumped. But we do not have to worry about feeling; that comes later. If we can know what God is, that itself is loving God. To know is to love, or, vice versa, to love is to know. The very act of knowing is the act of loving—whether neighbor or God.

Carved in the stone wall of the main building at the University of Texas, and over the doors of many churches as well as educational institutions, is a line from the Book of John, "Know the truth, and the truth shall make you free." It does not say that the truth alone is going to make anybody free. The instruction is that if we "know" or experience the truth it will make us free. The closer we come to the knowledge of pure truth, the closer we are to having pure freedom. Whenever we have a truthful formula for any endeavor we have successful results and are free of failure and ignorance. Potentially there is a perfect formula or perfect truth about every activity, thing, or person on earth. This ultimate, infinite, unchanging truth is God. Our job is to find some way to relate to it.

As man is finite, we have the almost impossible task of trying to comprehend infinity. But we can think of God in the equation of life as being like the x in an algebra problem. Accepting that there is an x, a sublime truth beyond our comprehension, we can start to become free of our limited concept of life. When we work out the answer we then know what x is itself. To say that God does not exist because it is unknown is like saying x does not exist because the solution hasn't been found.

It is popular today to say that God is dead. Many men, mentally trapped into mere intellectual dialectics, have tried to say that God has ceased to exist because the limited concepts of truth are not adequate for the present generation. If what man means by the word "God" is his limited knowledge, then, indeed, God has ceased to exist just as the speed of the horse has ceased to be the top speed of transportation, just as the candle has ceased to be the best source of light for dispelling darkness. So to arrive at an alive God we must first dispel some of the limited concepts of God.

The stumbling block that causes most people to limit God is the use of the label for God as "the Supreme Being." When they say, "I believe in a Supreme Being," they immediately conceive of God with shape and size. They cannot help it. Instead of feeling some sense of God as all being, everything, total and infinite, they form a mental picture of a being with size and shape. Some picture God as an oversized and imposing man, eloquently bearded and with flowing robes enthroned in the heavens, others as a kindly benevolent image of their father. If that were the case, then Jesus must have been mistaken when he said that God was within us, because a father with body would have to shrink pretty small to get inside.

Nevertheless, it is easy to see how man identified God with the father figure. Traditionally we look to our father for security, protection, guidance, and even discipline. But when, as today, so much of security, protection, and even an amount of food and medical aid come from the government, we do not relate to the father figure as we did in the past. Many of the young are unable to conceive of God as father any longer. It is not their fault because they do not relate to their own fathers in that manner.

When the Number One power in life was seen as the father, that image was used to picture God. Man has tried to give a visible form to his concept of power. Primitive people knew that the sun was necessary for their food; so they thought the sun was God. Other, lesser elements of daily life became many gods in the Pantheon of their needs. Since today money represents the power to buy food, companionship, health, and love, many people secretly or subconsciously see money as God. Some people believe that their security lies in their jobs, and they worship them. Some athletes believe that their strong healthy bodies will supply all their needs, and they worship the body. Many people today believe that they can solve anything with their minds, and the mind becomes their altar. These are all forms of idolatry, and anyone who is worshiping any single aspect of life is bowing down before graven images.

You can tell how man conceives of God by the way he prays. Whenever you see a man praying to God as though he would receive some special dispensation if he said the right words, lit the right candle, or went into the right church, you know that the man has a false picture of God. His concept of God is that there is a kind of heavenly dictator whom one must propitiate. But, if there were some kind of god who would withhold good from some and give it to others as the whim of his own will, that god would be a demonic invention that would make a mockery of life. There cannot be a god or a truth that applies just for one person or thing. There can be a power of truth that is concerned equally for all.

Then what is God? In its availability for all, God is the action of Grace in one's life. In this respect you might say God is Grace itself. Grace is like the sun, mathematics, the alphabet, or any impersonal principle of life that exists for one and all. Grace is the maintaining and sustaining cause of all life. Grace is God in action. That which restores our strength when we are exhausted, that which heals us when we are sick, that which directs us to the answer for our problems, that which creates beauty in the world, that which is always there to restore us, is God.

God is the whole of life. It is the whole that contains all the parts. It is the law of all creativity. It is the supreme intelligence maintaining and sustaining all of life. God is the presence, the light, and the life of all being. God is that invisible entity that makes our bodies function and restores them. God is the spirit of truth that lies within all men and things. It is the fulfillment. God is ever present, all knowing. It is personal and yet it is impersonal because it is all. God is the circle of life. When we talk about the different aspects of God or the different ways God affects our lives, we are talking of segments of the circle of life, love, and truth. We are not talking about God because God is the whole circle, not any one part. God can, therefore, be nothing but the whole circle, all of it. Human beings do not want so much life, truth, and love. The choice is too absolute, so they try to limit God in false concepts, but God is everything or else he is nothing. Only those who can rise above their limited vision of God can know God.

One Power

After arriving at an over-all sense of the totality of God, we must then make the next step of reconciling the invisible with the visible. It is difficult enough to reconcile the inequities of man's life with the invisible side of man, but we can manage that with a force of will or determination. It is much harder, however, to reconcile the all-knowing omnipresence of God with the catastrophes of life. We can say, "I know not to judge my neighbor by appearances; so I will love God by not judging life." But if we cannot arrive at some principle to sustain that idea, we will not succeed.

Man sees experiences in a moment of time, and he judges them as bad or good according to his interpretation of the moment. Often, when time has passed, he looks back and sees that he was wrong in what he thought at the time. Often what appears as destruction is only the process of creation. If one has a garden there comes a time when one must rip out some of the plants, cultivate the soil, and replant the garden. Then it can grow into greater glory. If someone walks in and sees the garden as part of it is being ripped up, he cannot possibly believe it is a good thing without the knowledge of the total picture. Actually there is only one power at work, and that is for good.

When a baby is cutting his teeth, there is pain and confusion for the baby, but the parent, from his deified position, knows that there is only a power of good operating for the growth of the child. The baby's teeth are growing as an act of Grace, and Grace is the only power operating. The parent does not judge the baby for crying, and the parent does not blame God for the child's growing. To love God is to know that there is no power apart from God's power.

When we believe that there are two powers operating in life we must find a way of reconciling them into oneness, and then we can become free of ignorance. Then we are loving God. A loose analogy can be made about the electric light. As an instrument, the light bulb itself is nothing but a bit of wire, glass, and such. There are negative and positive wires leading from the socket. If people thought that the positive current was good and the negative bad they would set about trying to eliminate the negative and would end up without any light. They would mistakenly be believing that the two powers were in conflict. Actually it is the polarity of these two currents that makes the light possible.

In the invisible where man can spiritually sense but not see, there is only one power. What appears humanly as duality is actually spiritual polarity.

The larger the potential force the more tempting it is to judge and the harder it is to reconcile the negative appearances. When there are only a few watts of electricity the negative and positive are easy to hook up. There is little danger if ignorance predominates and the truth is misused. If there is a half million watts of electricity it is much harder to harness, and much more destruction can come to those who approach it with ignorance. But, once harnessed, this polarity of plus and minus could produce enough light to light a whole city. The use of atomic energy can be seen as an example. Atomic energy could destroy the world, or its energy could be harnessed to feed and house the whole world. Because of this great concentration of power we are more easily tempted to judge it.

At a personal level, some people judge that there is a built-in conflict between man and woman. Here too this conflict is polarity, and not duality. Generally the man has the power to create supply, to make a home, or to overcome material bondage. At some times, if the woman or family did not supply the need the man would not go out and fulfill himself as a creator. This is not duality for each side is necessary in the creative processes, just as it takes both man and woman to produce a child. Polarity not duality.

Another mistake that is made in trying to reconcile two powers into oneness is that people think reconciling means they should make the apparently opposite powers be the same. In the human scene we always have bad and good. Trying to say they are the same is not reconciling them. The plus and minus currents in the light bulb are equal in importance, but they are not the same.

For instance, for centuries women have been considered inferior to men because their capacity to procreate made them more earthbound, more vulnerable, more prone to judging material bad and good. Now, the universal consciousness has risen to the point where it is realized that women are not spiritually inferior. In its place many are making another mistake. In the guise of equality they perpetrate sameness. Many feel that equality means women should assume the masculine role, that they should have the same powers and abilities as man. The ignorance of this position has caused great sexual and social confusion. In time, the truth will evolve and appearances will be reconciled. Man and woman will be seen as equals spiritually but necessarily not similar physically or emotionally. Then man and woman will stand side by side, equally necessary, equally worthy, but each fulfilling his necessarily dissimilar role on the visible scene. One power of life is operating.

The Absence of Truth

It is confusing enough to try to see that what looks like destruction is often part of creation, but there is one more step to take in order to be able to reconcile life into oneness. It is the most difficult of all. To take this step requires a great effort of double thinking. We often hear, "Why did God let that happen?" when tragedy strikes a family, when there is an automobile accident, or a child drowns in a swimming pool. But God, or truth, did not let it happen. It was the absence of truth on the scene that was causing the tragedy.

When you take a light into the darkness the light does not overcome a power of darkness. Where the light is there just isn't any darkness. There were not two powers, a power of darkness and a power of light. Darkness has no power. If darkness had power then pitch darkness would be able to overcome a small candle. But the candle has the power of light and, no matter how strong the darkness where the presence of the candle's flame is, the darkness is dispelled. When ignorance is present, when truth is absent, there is power in that ignorance but it is only a false power. The minute truth is present ignorance has no power. Ignorance only borrows its power from truth.

It is confusing to call God the only power because the word "power" implies a power over something. It would be more accurate to say that God is the only cause or truth of being. Then when we see the appearance of evil and destruction we can shake ourselves out of the belief that God is losing some kind of struggle against another power. When a man is suffering from the d.t.'s we do not try to erase the snakes he is fighting in his sick mind, or chase away the pink elephants. We reconcile the appearance, we do not fight the evil; rather, we sober the man up, wake him from his state of ignorance. Then the false powers disappear of themselves. Rather than fight the ignorance, we reveal the truth. We know that God is the only true cause and that is what it means to love God. If we can look straight at the conditions and know that when truth is revealed the forces of evil will be powerless, that the evil conditions are there only because of the absence of the conscious awareness of truth, we have a foundation upon which we can stand.

Mankind as a whole is still in a partially hypnotic state in the process of waking up. When the universal consciousness of man is completely awake, when mankind is free of ignorance, when man knows himself and his fellow man with pure righteous judgment, there will be no more ignorance. When there is no more ignorance, he will see that there is only one power operating in the universe. He will love God, and only the harmony of peace and truth will remain.

CHAPTER 8

THE PLAY AND THE PLOT

Shakespeare said that all the world's a stage, and all the men and women merely players. If he had lived today he probably would have said, less eloquently, that all the world was a soap opera. Actually, we can learn to take this world a lot more easily if we can indeed see it as a drama and have a sense of humor about it. Having a sense of humor is considered a prime virtue for man, and that is no accident. If a man can smile at himself and the world, he has not lost sight of the realization that life is two-sided. One is "man of earth" and "man of Christ," and when we never lose sight of this double aspect we stay in balance.

Whenever the balance is lost, objectivity is lost, and man becomes useless to himself and everyone else. When anger rises up in a man to the point where he loses his detachment, his sense of humor, or the double vision of himself, it spills over inside him and he is not himself. Whenever an athlete tightens up and loses his detachment, he can no longer perform at his best. An actor on the stage must be there with "tears in his eyes, distraction in his aspect" but at the same time another side of him must be able to say, "Someone coughed in the balcony, raise your voice, pick up your cues." If he loses this double function he becomes useless as an actor.

The theater as an imitation of life can teach us many things whereby we can parallel life with spiritual development. We can see why the world is attracted to theater and where the theater's power lies. We can understand mankind as the world cast and how he performs in the world drama. We can see the theatrical illusion of life itself and can attain an understanding of the plot and its fulfillment.

The Attraction of Theater

Through the centuries man has felt an attraction to the theater. Whenever man is attracted to anything, it is because that thing holds some key to the source of life. Man has come to recognize the power in theater but not necessarily to understand it, and like any other power, this power of theater can be used to perpetuate ignorance as well as truth.

The secret lies in the fact that when theater achieves its purpose, it has created a sense of life on the stage that is so real the audience is caught up in it. Man forgets he is sitting in a theater. For a moment he accepts the reality of the life he is beholding. He drops the personal awareness of life that he had when he entered the theater, and he accepts the life the performers are presenting. If the writers, producers, and performers have achieved their goal, have reached a high degree of the truth of their profession, the performance is a success and, for a moment, the audience forgets its own limited existence. If the performance is not successful, it is quite obviously because it has failed to create the illusion of reality. The members of the audience do not accept the performance; they squirm in their seats, cough, and even walk out.

The theater shows us that if man's consciousness can create a dream on the stage that is real enough for the audience to accept it as reality, then man has the power within his consciousness to break the twenty-four-hour-a-day dream of his own limitations. There is no more reality in the dream caused by our ignorance about life than there is in the one happening on the stage. Most of all it shows that man's imagination can free him and create a better world. The fearful reality which we accept in life—of war, of poverty, and of man's inhumanity to man—may not be any more real than the fearful tragedy we respond to in the theater. We can ring down the curtain and become free from that bondage by an act of our own will or creativity. Comedy shows us that despite the tragedy that may have accompanied us as we walked into the theater, we can laugh and become free.

This is the truth and the appeal behind all great art. Paintings exalt man because they reveal man's ability to express truth and beauty. They show that man can not only comprehend beauty, but that he can also create a greater beauty than that which he has had thrust upon him by life. Great novels lift man into a higher sense of truth, and reveal the fact that man is made to have "dominion" over all matter on earth. It makes no difference whether the subject of art or theater is of a tragic or a comic nature. Either frees man if it has lifted him for a moment out of his own limitations. This moment of respite is a moment of pause from his limited sense of self, and it prepares him for the moment of Grace that is always there waiting to express itself.

When theater and art are consciously recognized as a means to lift men to a higher level of consciousness, to change his vibration, to free him—not by what they preach but by what they do—they will reach a height of expression never before seen, and can do more to free man than any institution man has contrived. Grace is always acting in man's life, always waiting to be freed to express itself; so if man's attention can be taken from his own ignorance for just a moment, Grace can break through and perform untold miracles.

Theater and religion have a similarity and an appeal to mankind that is not accidental. The power of both originates from the same cause. Theater and religion both activate the imagination of man, and it is man's imagination that creates the forms of life. In turn, the imagination lifts man and life. It can lift one into freedom.

The Cast of Characters

Human beings are the actors on the stage of the world. Mankind, the audience, sees the parts the actors are playing but the roles do not represent the truth about the actors themselves. The only thing the world sees is a limited, relatively one-sided performance taking place. Like an actor in a summer stock company, a man plays many different parts, and we judge him by the ones we see.

The audience never sees an actor without one of his make-ups on, one of his faces. Laurence Olivier may appear on the stage behind the beard and make-up of Othello, but we, by an act of righteous judgment, realize that behind the mask is the true man who has very little to do with the outer action. Otherwise we would rush up on the stage to stop him when Othello strangles his wife.

A thousand people may know you, or think they do. One says, "Oh yes, he is that grouchy man I had to wake up early the other morning." Another says, "Oh yes, he is that kind man I saw helping an old lady across the street." Someone might say, "Oh yes, I knew her ten years ago. She is that attractive girl with a divine figure." Or another says, "Oh yes, I know her. She is that squatty little woman with the double chin." All of them may be talking about one of your performances, one aspect of the truth of you, but not one of them knows the whole truth of you so long as he sees you with human judgment, on the stage.

Actually, back in the dressing room, where the world doesn't come, the actors take off their make-up and all go out for a cup of coffee. At that point they are not stars and bit players, not villains and heroes. There are no lines that they have to speak and no human plot. They just are. At that moment, knowing both what it is to be on the stage and off it, they are judging with righteous judgment and love is present.

On the other hand, both the audience and the actor get in trouble when they lose the double thread and forget that what is taking place is a performance and not reality. There was a motion picture called *A Double Life* where an actor was playing Othello in a long run. Little by little he lost sight of reality until he thought he was, indeed, Othello and strangled his wife. Pretty corny but far too true to life to be dismissed. When she was performing in a play called *The Lark*, the actress Julie Harris fell on stage and cut her lip. They had to pull the curtain down and bandage the lip before she could finish the play. Shortly thereafter she said, "You know, that was my fault. I forgot I was acting."

The troubles we have as humans—fear, sexual frustration, deprivation, loneliness and the like—are the grease paint on the surface of our being. When we are off the stage and cleansed, these fears and deprivations are no more. We are pure and our true faces show. When we want something of another person, when we think Othello has something we want, we have been tricked into believing that an Othello really exists. By desire we are tricked into the illusion.

When we want nothing from the characters or the plot, when we are in harmony with the characters and the plot, we are fulfilling both of the two commandments. We are judging righteously and we are loving God.

The Theatrical Illusion of Life

When the illusion of theater is successful, we have forgotten we are sitting in our seats. When we are believing in what we are seeing, we are possessed by what is taking place. Whenever in life we are dominated by the illusion of fear, lack, or any other bondage, we are soul possessed by material illusion. When we are not under the spell of illusion, we are truly our selves—free, unhypnotized, and one with God. Therefore, whenever we are not free, whenever we believe that there are evil powers operating in our lives, we are soul possessed. If our sense of security is based on a person, a job, or on any finite thing, we are soul possessed by that situation. If we withhold an action because of fear or because we are afraid of how another person will react, we are soul possessed by that situation or person.

From the time we are born, from the time we enter this theater, we are either being possessed or having to stand guard to keep from being possessed. Whenever we read a newspaper we are in danger of being soul possessed by the fear the headlines project. Whenever we are warned on television of the possibility of contracting some disease, we become possessed if we are driven to fear. A free un-possessed person is one who follows Jesus' instruction, "Call no man on earth your father." As long as we look for our good to any person, place, or thing in the human world we are possessed by that person, place, or thing. But if we look to God, the source of all being, for everything, we are free.

Because this soul possession is so total to most humans, the Oriental religions claim that the whole world is illusory. They say that when man awakes or experiences Nirvana he is free of the illusion. They feel that the illusion is so total that when man awakes there is no world left at all. It is easy to see why they feel that way. Man sees all matter through his very limited senses. His view is so distorted that it is almost completely illusory. In that respect, whenever he believes that things are purely as he sees them, he is being soul possessed by the material view. If he sees things in terms of consciousness manifesting itself in form, he is not. At any rate, the difference between the Oriental illusion of life and the Occidental point of view is this: the Oriental believes that life, like a stage play, is dream and when one wakes up, the dream, the play, the world ceases to exist; the Occidental believes that something is actually taking place on this world stage, that there is a material reality. He can believe that his opinion of what is here is so distorted by human judgment that it is almost illusory, but he does believe that something is here. In this respect the Christian comes close to the Oriental because he realizes that he must not judge by appearances, for if he does he is soul possessed by ignorance.

All the mistakes, all the tricks, all the temptations that fool man into believing he is cut off exist like a fog wrapped around the earth ready to take possession of man's mind. This universal ignorance is not a personal possession of any one man. No single man invented it any more than anyone invented integrity or honesty, but one can come under its illusion and be possessed by it if one loses the sense of righteous judgment, if one forgets how to love. The whole collection of ignorances that possess mankind is called "universal ignorance."

When we go into the theater, we know what we are doing and we take our chances. The illusion can trap us, but it can also lift us. We go to the theater in order to have an expansion of consciousness. We want to experience and to grow. As long as we are anchored in the realization that there is only one power we won't be tricked. It takes double thinking in the theater as well as in life. We might be tempted to judge some play as being dirty or depressing. We might say, "What does he have to put all that stuff on the stage for," and through our judgment miss seeing how the characters in the play are undergoing the ripping and tearing necessary for expanding consciousness. If we walk out on the play in disapproval, we might miss our own chance to expand.

Creativity, growth, expansion of consciousness always take a certain amount of what looks like destruction. When man becomes free from slavery, and when opportunity is offered to the masses, there is always enormous upheaval. Many complain about the upheavals that are apparent in today's social revolution, but perhaps they are all necessary for forcing an expansion of consciousness which is needed.

Many view with alarm the American upheaval in the area of marriage and sex. At the same time they close their eyes to the archaic practices in some of the old cultures. There the woman is automatically relegated to the position of baby maker alone. She is kept in the home, and is denied even the full companionship of the man. It has even been noticed that our American youth are exploded into life by the habit of doing ten different things at once —studying with one eye, looking at the television set with the other, and listening to hi-fi. Because of this forced expansion of consciousness our youth are more at ease and more productive in this mechanical age than those brought up in more simple rural backgrounds. The senses have been stretched to the point where American youth can cope with the complicated needs of a machine age that demands the coordination of many different senses at once.

The Plot and Fulfillment

The plot in the theater of life looks like one of creativity and destruction, but it is actually the same old prodigal son story that leads to creation. It is said the fundamental plot is, "Boy meets girl, boy loses girl, boy gets girl." We start from home, we lose our way, and we consciously find our way back.

In the double path of life we have been told that there comes a time when we must choose a plot line, a path we wish to tread: the spiritual or the material. We say we come to a "Y" in the road and must decide. Now it is revealed that it is just the opposite. We come to a "Y" in the road; that is when the two sides come together, when we can reconcile the material and the spiritual into one path.

Today, we hear some people extol the virtues of conformity, and others the virtues of being noncomformist. This is the day when both must come together, for both have virtues *and* ignorances. The mystery is that the virtues of one correct the ignorances of the other.

Our conventional society knows the importance of civic responsibility, concern for one's neighbor, and even the need for creating forms of organization to the betterment of cooperative industry. Yet conventional society often sits in judgment on those who do not conform. It limits individual freedom, it forces the continuation of organization even after the organization has served its purpose; it perpetuates hypocrisy, for man is unable to live completely by law.

The Bohemian world frees man not by sitting in judgment, not by forcing him to conform, but by letting each individual work out his own salvation according to his own evolvement. Often one finds more potential saints in a beatnik coffee house than in a great cathedral, because those in the coffee house are searching. The Bohemian may be searching in the wrong place, but he is searching. The conformist may have so formed his life as to be immobile; he may have pasted his life together by rising at seven, working till six, bridge on Monday, bowling on Tuesday, and so on, with no time to think or listen for the word of God within. These are the walking dead.

On the other hand, the Bohemian often has no consideration for others, no sense of responsibility for his fellow man. Often he dissipates his God-given creative forces in ways that render him useless to man and to himself.

When mankind arrives at the "Y" in the road, when the conformists cease judging the nonconformists, when the nonconformists cease judging conformity, and both realize their need for each other—then there will be harmony on earth. Whether it is seen in terms of man and woman, conformist and nonconformist, Occidental and Oriental, weak and strong or, ultimately, spiritualistic and materialistic—to be free, we must have and know both.

Man's goal, the plot of life, is to attain balance and wholeness. If only one end of the rope of life is secured, with the other end dangling in space, one can never keep balance because one can never relate where one is to the desired place of balance. When both ends are secure, when man thoroughly understands his spiritual side and his human side, he can walk the tightrope of life. Knowing both sides, man can know on which side to lean most heavily to keep balance. Those who realize they are spending too much time thinking of material matters can spend more time seeking spiritual balance. Those who tend easily to go off into the clouds can concentrate on more practical matters. But first we must know the world of man to know the world of God, and the world of God to know the world of man. The human mind is the stage on which the drama takes place. The setting for our drama is the world. The world is our monastery. Man need not go off into a monastery in order to hurry the processes of evolvement and expansion. He believes that by intensive study and prayer he will come more quickly to inner freedom, he finds instead that human nature follows him right into the monastery. Human personalities give him more trouble than they ever did because he sees them under the microscope of proximity. He thinks that by denying himself material things he will break their hold on him, but it is often exactly the opposite.

The world is our monastery, our stage set. If we accept being part of the cast as a chance to learn how to love people by not judging them according to what they do on the stage, we can learn to see the hand of God in every activity. We must wrestle with the substance of life, with the grease paint, the costumes, and all the props. Only by our refusal to turn our backs on the materials and substance of life can we know them and become free.

In his desperate desire to convince the world of this, of the necessity of knowing the world of matter in order to find the spiritual whole, Pierre Teilhard de Chardin cried:

"Son of earth, steep yourself in the sea of matter, bathe in its fiery waters, for it is the source of your life and your youthfulness.

"You thought you could do without it because the power of thought has been kindled in you? You hoped that the more thoroughly you rejected the tangible, the closer you would be to spirit: that you would be more divine if you lived in the world of pure thought, or at least more angelic if you fled the corporeal? Well, you were like to have perished of hunger.

"You must have oil for your limbs, blood for your veins, water for your soul, the world of reality for your intellect. . . ."

And

"Son of man, bathe yourself in the ocean of matter; plunge into it where it is deepest and most violent; struggle in its currents and drink of its waters. For it cradled you long ago in your preconscious existence; and it is that ocean that will raise you up to God."*

* *Hymn of the Universe* (New York: Harper & Row, 1965), pp. 63-64, 65. Used by permission of the publisher.

CHAPTER 9

THE SERPENT'S TRICK AND THE GREAT LIE

The kingdom of heaven could be right here, right now, if it were not for a trick that has been played on mankind. Man first got tricked in the Garden of Eden. Though Jesus did not fall for that trick which has put blinders on the eyes of most of mankind, there has been a lie about him that has perpetuated the trick right up until this moment.

The trouble actually started with Adam and Eve. We are told that Eve was tempted by an apple. Some people say that desire was the villain. Others have said that disobedience was the problem. But take a close look at the Scripture. The serpent said, "Eat, and then your eyes will be opened, and ye shall be as the gods." In other words, he tricked Eve with a direct appeal to her lack of belief in herself, to her self-doubt, or to a feeling of guilt. The serpent might as well have said, "You're not good enough. Open your eyes to your own inadequacies. Look at your faults, and, by all means, feel guilty."

When man accepted guilt he began to sit in judgment, calling everything bad or good. It is not far wrong to say that this was the fall of man because every human judgment separated him further and further from happiness and peace. The doctrine of original sin came into being as an attempt to explain this fall. But today it is not necessary to make it sound mysterious or supernatural. Man does have an original basic problem, but there is a perfectly rational explanation of the problem. Man is born with a dilemma, and unless he understands the basis of it the dilemma can trick him into feeling guilty. Man is born with finite size and shape. He has limited capacities as a human. But he is in a completely untenable position. He is finite; however, he is able to sense an infinity beyond his finite capacity. Man came from the infinite source of all being, and because he has a spiritual faculty it is possible for him to sense that infinity. From birth, man is plagued with an inner drive to express as much of infinity as he can.

Those who have had a glimpse of the potential that is lying dormant within themselves, in any man for that matter, feel the most guilty when they do not express it. The people who brag continuously are actually the most tricked by guilt. Their bragging really says, "See what I have done. I really am all right. I really am one with the source. I don't have to feel guilty." The more a man sees the infinity of his potential capacities, the more guilt he feels, the more he is driven. Man's unbalanced desire for money, fame, and great power comes from a sense of guilt. He senses that he has that within him which is all-powerful and fulfilling, and he thinks having the tangible benefits of money and fame proves it. When he has the rewards, he feels, he will not have to justify himself or feel guilty.

Guilt puts man under the bondage of human judgment and the first law of human nature. It puts him under law; he becomes earthbound. Guilt blocks the flow of Grace, and freedom is lost. As long as man is tricked into feeling guilty, he depends on his mind to live his life for him and to tell him what is right and wrong so that he will not have to feel more guilty and cut off.

Today guilt is used as a whip. Once discipline was mainly physical, but as this is a mental age, discipline has now become mental. The mind knows that man does not want to feel guilty and cut off from God; so it uses guilt to punish. This takes many forms. A mother tells a child, "Now why did you do that, darling; you made mother very unhappy." By telling the child he had made mother unhappy the mother has used the child's love for her as a whip of guilt. Society advertises the desirability of conformity and tricks man into a position where it can punish him with guilt if he gets out of line. We individually advertise the halo around our own heads as a bid to make others feel guilty by comparison. Even if we set such a pace for ourselves that others in our family or profession cannot keep up with us, we are possibly tricking them into feeling guilty. Whenever we act to make another feel guilty, we are serpents using the serpent's trick to separate others from God. And those who live with guilt are choking for life.

Think of anyone you admire and want to be around. It will probably be someone who never makes you feel guilty. In fact, it will probably be someone who causes you to feel guiltless, loved. That is why the institution of the confessional came about. Man discovered that after he confessed and was purged of guilt he felt a miraculous sense of freedom. The minute guilt was removed, Grace was felt, and he was no longer tricked by guilt.

The Untricked Jesus

Jesus was not tricked by guilt. When it is said that Jesus redeemed mankind, it could be said that Jesus saw through the temptation to feel guilty. Eve was tempted by the serpent's words, but Jesus responded differently when Satan tried to tempt him. Scripture reports that Satan said, "If ye be the Son of God, turn this stone into bread." The temptation was not to turn stones into bread. The trick lay in the words, "If ye be the Son of God." In other words, Go on, prove you are the Son of God; go on, use your power of consciousness to manifest more security. But Jesus was secure in the knowledge of his own being and in righteous judgment. He did not have to prove anything to anyone. He rejected the temptation with the words, "Get thee behind me, Satan." That is to say, Get thee into the past ignorance for I have no need to prove my oneness with truth and being. I *am*.

Had he qualified that truth, had he explained with guilt, "I am not one with truth as you see me. This material form is not one with truth," the world would not have had him crucified. Everyone else felt a sense of guilt; so if he had implied that he too was tricked there would have been no need to shut him up. No one would have feared his truth. Had he qualified his human existence, he would have continued man's sense of duality and perpetuated the dualistic belief in a material world and separate spiritual one. He so saw his oneness with the truth of being that he guiltlessly claimed, "I and the Father are one."

The ignorance of man is always fearful of the guiltlessness of a creative consciousness. Ignorance resists change in order to preserve itself. Jesus was the ultimate threat to all ignorance. If the truth in Jesus' consciousness became the truth of the universal consciousness, then universal ignorance itself would be eliminated for all time. Ignorance had to do everything it could to blind man to truth, and it did its best and most subtle job in blinding man to the truth about Jesus.

Ignorance created a Jesus that was not a whole man. It said that Jesus did not have the conflicts and problems that other men had. It said that Jesus never made any mistakes. It said that he was complete right from his birth on. It implied that he was not human, that he was really not a person.

But Jesus was a personal man, and personal freedom for each man is bound up in the truth of his individual being. Jesus was a whole man. At each level—body, mind, and spirit—his life demonstrated the perfection of each aspect of life. Man was quite right in his desire to revere Jesus as God on earth for he was indeed the revelation of truth on earth. As the product of the truth of what man can be, he is entitled to the label of "The Son of God." We are quite right to say he was both man and God, for he was truth expressed as man. Man is quite right in saying that one must let Jesus Christ enter one's life because man will never find freedom until that same consciousness that was in Jesus is his consciousness. We are quite right in saying that Jesus is our personal saviour, because it is the example of his person that can save man. Man is quite right in exalting his image, meditating on his life, and listening to the source of his being, for that is truth expressed at both the visible and invisible levels. When man feels a personal love for Jesus, he is simply responding at the personal level, and man should respond at all levels.

The Lie Exposed

Then where did man go wrong? What is the lie that confused mankind? The lie has to do with what man means by perfection. The original sin of guilt was caused by man's misinterpretation of perfection. He proposed something called perfection and measured all judgment by it: perfection was good, and imperfection was bad.

Perfection does exist, but not according to man's limited comprehension of its meaning. Man can never see perfection. When it is based on flawlessness, it cannot exist. You can put a million similar objects under a microscope and no two are alike. Perfection is relative. To expect any two things to be exactly alike is to doom them to failure and imperfection. To expect any two people to understand a doctrine in exactly the same manner is to place them under law and doom them to failure. Perfection does exist in terms of an ultimate spiritual principle of what life is and should be, but man can only sense this—he cannot comprehend perfection with his finite mind.

The great lie is—when man, in his ignorance, misinterpreted perfection and then claimed that Jesus was perfect, all those who tried to follow Jesus were doomed to failure. Man said, "Here is perfect, flawless Jesus. Be like him or feel guilty." That Jesus never existed, could not exist.

Jesus was the word made flesh. That means he inhabited this finite world where flaws exist. When man painted a picture of Jesus with no humanity as though he never stumbled, never fell, never cried, and never contradicted himself, we were tricked out of ever seeing the truth of Jesus' life.

Until the time of his ascension, Jesus showed his humanity in multiple ways. When he was tired and sick in spirit, he needed, as you and I do, to go off to a mountain-top to get refreshed. When life was too much for him, he said, "Let this cup pass from me." This is the way for all mankind. Yet man has been taught that it is wrong to have moments of fear, to stumble and fall, to have what look like flaws. If one interprets "flaws" as being problems or irregularities, Jesus was perfect in spiritual terms, but he was not flawless. To expect man to be flawless condemns him to defeat. Defeat brings guilt. When man feels guilty, he can never dare to see the truth of himself as being one with God.

No sooner had the Master said that man should not resist evil than he turned around and chased the money-changers out of the temple. It was the priests of that same temple who went to the authorities and had Jesus crucified. From this it seems that Jesus was imperfect because he caused himself to be crucified.

Jesus preached that God was the only power. It seems confusing, then, that he would believe that the money-changers had the power to disrespect his Father's house. But had Jesus never been crucified, he could never have proved the power of spirit over matter; he could never have proved the unreality of death. The miracle of the Master's life is that, though he completely knew the lack of reality in the human picture, he would or could participate at that level and thereby free man from the bondage of the illusory aspect of matter.

Though Jesus knew that God was fully operating in the lives of all mankind, he nevertheless set about to save the world. He took on a sense of personal responsibility, and that seemed to eliminate God. He even anticipated his crucifixion, and that seemed to contradict his teaching of "take no thought for the morrow." But, just as the light bulb needs both the negative and positive to produce the perfection of light, there was actually no contradiction in Jesus' acts for by these acts he demonstrated the totality of God. His seeming errors were his bridge to mankind, his cross, his virtue, and his human mortification as well.

Jesus' sense of personal responsibility made it possible for him to be betrayed. By saying, "I have come to save the world," he made it possible for the ignorance of man to think it could stop the world from being saved if it killed the person of Jesus. But when Jesus was betrayed, the door was opened to set free all men from the necessity of condemning their own sense of personal responsibility, their own seeming flaws. Men could realize that they too had that within themselves, as Jesus did, that could overcome the world.

When institutions and churches were created which, in their zeal to teach the divinity of Jesus, alleged Jesus was humanly flawless and told men that they should be like Jesus or feel guilty, they placed mankind in bondage. Love frees one from bondage, but, in the name of love, those institutions fraudulently fed men with a diet of guilt or hate. Under the name of the Master, man was whipped into seeing himself as sinning, finite, helpless man. As we imagine ourselves to be, so we become.

On the other hand, there have been religious movements which realized the spirit of man was already perfect. But then the human mind of the individuals in the movements tricked them into all kinds of physical excesses which doomed the sects to the worst kind of animalistic and egotistical failure. If man is to err on one side or the other, it is best that he err in seeing himself as too human. But now is the day when the double aspect of man can be understood and kept in balance, and Jesus' example is ready for the mass of mankind to follow.

The truth of both aspects—that human man is imperfect and that spiritual man is perfect—has existed down through the centuries of theological discussion, but the overemphasis placed on the finite, error-filled aspect of man has thrown the truth out of balance. That which was meant to be a power for freedom became instead, because of the distortion, a power of bondage for mankind.

If we are discouraged in our inability to keep the two sides balanced, it might be good to realize that it took Jesus about thirty years to grow into mature Christhood. It took him the three more years of his ministry to rise completely out of humanhood. Even after the resurrection the scars of humanity remained, and only at the full ascension was his job done, his task completed. If we look at the years of his ministry without its fulfillment in the resurrection and ascension, we can make a case for his failure and point out contradictions present in his story. But when we accept his humanity and analyze the steps of his life without losing sight of the resurrection, we can see the spiritual perfection of his being.

The Thorn in the Flesh

To be perfect man, one must have flaws. One must have imperfections to keep one humble, pure, and truly man. Without imperfections there could be no attainment. Jesus was perfect because he had these apparent inconsistencies. Only by realizing that there are perfections where faults appear, do we realize the kingdom of heaven here and now. When we realize that imperfections, thorns in the flesh, are part of the perfection of life, we can see that there is no power apart from God.

Were there no imperfections, there would be nothing to spur man on to creation. Were there no unfulfilled desire motivating him, man would not move. It is hard for us, who have been trained to believe it evil to have imperfections, to see the value of flaws. Nevertheless, in the twelfth chapter of II Corinthians we read: "Lest I should be exalted above measure through the abundance of the revelations, there was given to me a thorn in the flesh, the messenger of Satan to buffet me. . . . For this I besought the Lord that it might depart from me. And he said unto me, My grace is sufficient for thee: for my strength is made perfect in weakness." Translated into modern thought, that statement might read: "Because I was born with the ability to create, I was given a flaw in my character or life to keep me pushing and creating. It was a devilish frustration. I turned to religion to try to get free, and I found that the purpose of the frustration was that it would keep driving me until I attained full realization of my oneness with truth, until I got off the seesaw, until I realized that the Grace of truth was sufficient for me. And then I would know the real truth—that I create in direct ratio as I realize it isn't little me who is doing it, but the oneness I have with the source of life."

Often the most outstanding and worthy people have reached their prominence because they hid a sharp thorn in the flesh, the overcoming of which drove them to their great creative effort. In the past forty years there has been more scandal about public and important figures than ever before. This is because in the past forty years the communications media have had the power to expose the full story of men. People lament that we have no heroes today. If the past had had the X-ray eye of television, radio, newspaper, and the telephone to focus such microscopic attention on man, we would find that there never were any flawless heroes.

It is a law of life that in every great and constructive man while he is most creative there is a flaw, a thorn in the flesh. And, probably the bigger the man, the bigger the thorn. It is the nature of being human to have flaws, differences, drives, needs, and the polarity of one's nature. When we realize this, we no longer need to feel guilty and deceitful because we are hiding flaws of our own. We can be guiltless and judgeless. We can realize that it is possible to be like Jesus because Jesus was like us.

While realizing this we must, however, keep in mind the realization that we do not want to fall into the trap of believing that there is virtue in suffering, that man *should* suffer. There is no true virtue in ignorance, error, or suffering. Like the power of evil, it borrows its power from truth, but is not a real power. If you make a mistake enough times, you are indeed driven to find the truth and become free. There is no real virtue in saying mistakes are good though they do lead us to the truth. To say there is virtue in suffering would be to put that into imagination and create more ignorance, not less.

Jesus symbolized the perfect man: perfect balance, perfect equilibrium. Not perfect, good in a one-sided way, not separate and aloof from man, but real and containing infinite so-called bad and good, material and spiritual, in perfect balance. He proved that one man had within him a model of the entire universe. By understanding his example, individual man can become free. Therefore the consciousness of the entire universe can find freedom. The symbol of the cross demonstrates the vertical and the horizontal in perfect balance.

As long as man beholds Jesus with a false sense of perfection, a kind of perfection that is impossible for man to attain, a wall is created that makes freedom and fulfillment utterly impossible. As long as the healings performed by Jesus are a special dispensation for him, rather than a natural effect of his spiritualized state of consciousness, the secret of healing is lost. As long as his life and ultimate demonstration of transcendence are taught and accepted as a unique experience for Jesus alone, his life is a failure. He taught that we should "go and do likewise," that "greater works shall ye do" because he has given us the tools of consciousness to work with. In every way he taught of joint heirship. "We are the heir and joint heir with Christ in God." The miracle of his whole mission is that he shows us the way in being like us.

The Second Easter

In the Scriptures there are accounts of two Easter experiences. The first—that of the Master's death and resurrection—is so dazzling that we miss the importance of the Second Easter. Actually, the Second Easter is more significant for you and me and more personally relevant.

The twelfth chapter of Acts recounts that Herod, the same king who was powerful enough to put Jesus on the cross, wanted to please the same people he was trying to please when he crucified Jesus. This time, at Easter, to please those who wanted to put an end to the Christian message, he put Peter in prison intending to crucify him as well.

Though in prison, guarded by squadrons of soldiers, within the consciousness of Peter was that which freed him from material bondage. He was subject to the same power that had imprisoned Jesus, the same power that had been able to put Jesus on the cross, yet he walked out of prison without using force. He too was resurrected. By walking free from the same conditions which had caused Jesus' crucifixion, Peter demonstrated a resurrection as real as that of the master, and showed it was not a unique possibility for Jesus alone.

Upon his freedom, Peter went to the house where the disciples were gathered, and they were amazed at his accomplishment. These were Jesus' star pupils; they had witnessed countless demonstrations by the Master, including his final one. Yet they were surprised when Peter, one of them, demonstrated the same truth that Jesus had. If those who were on the spot did not accept the fact that the same possibility was there for them, it is small wonder that the world of mankind has so far not accepted it.

When Peter demonstrated that he too had the "mind that was in Christ Jesus," he demonstrated Jesus' greatest miracle of all. He demonstrated that Jesus not only had the truth for himself, but that he could pass it on to his students. He proved that Jesus' example was not a freak experience of one man, but the guide to freedom for all mankind.

At the door of the house of the disciples where they were "amazed" on seeing his attainment of freedom, Peter refused to enter. He said, "Now we have the key and the proof for all mankind. Let us now go show the world."

To expect perfection in human terms is to deny Jesus Christ and is to insure a life lived by the mind, by judgment, by duality, and by bondage. Expecting perfection, it is impossible to love, for love is expressed when one rises above the judgment of superior and inferior, of visible appearances, and when one sees the spiritual perfection of man or God. You can talk all you wish about loving another, but if you in any way make him feel guilty, you are hating him.

Expecting material perfection makes prayer impossible, for the very act of praying is the act of experiencing the release from the world of bad and good, of vice and virtue, of imperfection and perfection. To expect perfection, flawlessness in absolute human terms, would be to eliminate all human creativity. For every man who has ever created knows that he did not reach the perfection he was able to comprehend. Man knows the impossibility of creating perfection. If he thought he had to create perfection or be condemned, he would never even attempt to try to create at all.

It is impossible to accept God as the Infinite truth, ground, cause, and reality, and look at life in terms of good and bad. It is incomprehensible that man can accept such a statement and still turn right around and judge those around him in terms of their human perfection. Any time we judge, we are saying that there is another creation besides God's, that there is another reality. We are saying that man's finite mind is God, because it has the power to know that which is perfect and that which is not.

We, seeing our acceptance of the Great Lie, can turn within, listening quietly until that sense of truth within us says:

Judge not, lest ye be judged and be limited to your own imperfections. Lift up your eyes unto the hills, unto the high points of truth, from whence comes your freedom. Realize that the kingdom of heaven already is present when we are freed from looking into a future time expecting some human perfection. The kingdom is not to come; the only thing is for us to open our eyes and we will behold it right here where we once judged. Feel the freedom and joy you experience the minute your mind lets go of the burden of judging. Feel the freedom you experience when you realize that even the Master had what looked like human imperfections. Feel the freedom that comes when you realize you do not have to insult your mind by not accepting appearances, but that you can be free by looking at them and by knowing that you are tempted to judge them in human terms of good and bad, that you have been tempted to have to accept them with judgment. Now you can look at the faulty without condemning it, knowing that it has its place, perhaps needs betterment, but isn't less God, less good in its spiritual reality. Feel the power of forgiveness: any time when we no longer look for perfection in another we are forgiving them. Forgiveness takes place the minute you withdraw judgment; it isn't even necessary to apologize, for we have released the spiritual truth of the other's being. Now in this release, feel the joy or peace in the realization that there is only one being, one power, and one reality. We are feeling God. We are praying.

CHAPTER 10

THE WHAT AND
THE HOW

❧

Prayer is not a thing. It is an experience. The aim of prayer is to experience the reestablishment of Grace in one's life. Prayer is one's attempt to hook up with the source once more. No one is praying unless he is experiencing that contact.

The most pronounced fault with the Western world's approach to religion is that it so often leaves out the experience of God. The virtue of the Western world is that it has "the word." You might say the Christian message has the "what." On the other hand, the Oriental world has the "how." The value and techniques of contemplation—turning within to experience life and God—have been the main themes of most of the Oriental religions. They in turn have neglected the "what." Their relation with God has been intense, but they have neglected the love of the visible neighbor. When the "what" and the "how" are put together, not only will the experience be there, but also it

97

will have the power of the word behind it.

Let us first take a look at what prayer really is and can be. Then we can learn how to do it. First of all, it is as impossible to understand prayer as it is to understand God, but it works nevertheless, just as God influences our lives without our really understanding what God is. Next, as prayer is an experience and not a formula, it is best to get rid of the limited views in order to know what it is so that we can experience it.

Some people see God as a kind of benevolent boss in heaven, and for them prayer is a form of two-way conversation where they talk while God listens. The problem for them here is that they must then find the right words or right thoughts to please God. But if one sees God as all-knowing, all-wise, there is little value in trying to inform God of anything. If God is a universal principle for saint and sinner alike, there is no value in asking for anything, because God is not withholding anything. The danger in the kinds of prayers which necessitate there being a God and a petitioner is that this might cause one to feel separated from God. Actually, the value of prayer is in making one feel united with God.

Prayer is not something that takes place on the outside of a person. It is not necessary to go off to a holy mountain nor is it necessary to visit a particular church. Jesus warned us against trying to find prayer in a place. "The time is coming when you will worship the Father neither on this mountain, nor in Jerusalem" and "the time approaches, indeed it is already here, when those who are real worshippers will worship the Father in spirit and in truth. Such are the worshippers whom the Father wants. God is spirit, and those who worship him must worship in spirit and in truth." He also advised that we should retire within our closet, within ourselves, and there make contact. "Know the truth, and the truth shall make you free." One must "pray aright" and then prayer will be effective.

When Jesus said, "Ask what ye will in my name and it shall be done," he was saying that effective prayer had to be in the consciousness of truth, his name.

In order to keep from seeing prayer as something on the outside, some modern metaphysical teachings have come up with a number of new words to use instead of the word "prayer." One word they use is "treatment." Treatment was a concept of breaking through the false picture to get at the true. But this soon became a formula. It was no longer an experience and therefore lost its meaning. There began to be a treatment for every different situation, not too unlike the different gods primitive man had for every need, and this practice became idolatry. When one first prayed aright and experienced truth, a statement of truth came from the experience. But when the statement was used over and over again, it dried up and became merely an effect.

At one time ritualistic prayer, beauty, and pageantry could lift man beyond the sense of his own finite nature and could be a most valuable aid in helping him to realize his oneness with the impersonal creative source of all life. When ritual became heavy with tradition and law, when it covered itself with worldly extravagance and became a pageant of men's pride, it set the seal upon the separation and inadequacy of man. Eventually the denial of all ritual worked the same harm in reverse. A beautiful flower, a shining candle flame, a graceful spire reaching into the heavens can bring joy to the heart of a man as signs that the outer beauty comes from within the soul of man and deserves its place in the infinite expression of God, truth.

One of the paradoxes of life is that the very act of praying is an admission that we are imagining ourselves separate and apart from God while we are wishing to imagine ourselves one with God. God is the only creative truth of life, and since this truth is operating with a perfection, harmony, and fulfillment beyond our limited knowledge, anything that accomplishes the experience of truth, that brings us in communion with truth, is prayer. Anything of which we have not been formerly aware that brings harmony, peace, and joy into our lives is also prayer. Prayer is an experience. It is not an effect, a thing, a formula. Effects, formulas, and even words might be aids in helping us attain a state of prayer, but prayer itself is not accomplished unless contact is established in oneness with the *being*ness, *all*ness, and *is*ness of life.

When a man goes fishing and sits quietly by the water's edge, waiting silently, communing with nature and life, he makes an inner contact that refreshes and restores him. That is prayer for him. When a music lover sits in contemplation of a heavenly symphony until he feels release and contact, he is praying. When one takes a walk in the woods or views a beautiful sunset and experiences the oneness of life, one is praying. When one experiences the joy of healthy companionship, one is praying.

The Scriptures tell us we should "pray without ceasing." Yet man was duped into thinking he should constantly mumble prayers. Man's words are of little power, but the words of truth revealed within are infinite in power. Therefore, to pray without ceasing is to keep a listening ear open at all times.

Listening

The most valuable word to use for the correct meaning of prayer is the word "listening." The act of listening connotes withdrawing our attention from the visible scene, a turning within, a receptivity, an expectancy. It does not imply the use of the mind to tell God anything; it does not imply a petitioning or physical action. It is a realization that there is an infinite truth within. When we understand prayer as a listening to the still small voice, "Speak Father, thy servant heareth," we are acknowledging that within our own being we have the source which can and will guide and direct us.

The still small voice is always there, but our frequencies are jammed with the many false broadcasts of the human ego and sense of judgment. The voice of bad and good screams into our ears from the universal ignorance of life. It is our job to shut off the false judgment, and tune up the true. That is fulfilling the two commandments: first, seeing the neighbor with righteous judgment, second, seeing the truth of God, life. The activity of doing just that is the activity of prayer.

Whenever a problem presents itself, whenever there is a need for a sudden decision, whenever something starts to bother you, you can pray. You can say "Excuse me, I want to go listen for a bit." Then you can retire into a quiet place, sit still, get rid of your limited concepts, and open yourself to hear, sense, or feel that which is the right thing or answer according to Grace.

Oriental listening is symbolized by the word "meditation," and we can learn a great deal from the East on that subject. That is the "how" on which the Orient has concentrated. Although many in the East have been sidetracked by elaborate physical techniques of meditation, the initial realization of the importance of getting quiet and turning within is there. They explain that the goal of meditation is to "one-point" the mind. And indeed, when all thoughts are gone from the mind except the one thought or attention on God, one is ready and open to have truth reveal itself. Unfortunately many approach meditation in a way that misses the double thread of life. They think meditation is a kind of act of hitting oneself over the head with a hammer, a deadening of the mind, rather than a clearing of the false broadcasts of the mind so that it can be used properly by the truth within.

Techniques of meditation are not important in themselves. They are only helps in getting one into a listening attitude. Each person must actually find his own way. As we in the West are not used to sitting cross-legged all of our lives, for us it is advisable to find a comfortable chair where one can sit in a relaxed but healthy manner so that the body does not intrude itself. It is possibly good to close the eyes in order to keep out the limited view of the senses and in order to make concentration easier. It is good to breathe simply or rhythmically in order to feel relaxed and free of the body sense. Then we can gently direct our minds in contemplation.

It is wise, however, not to confuse "contemplation" with "meditation." Actually, contemplation leads into meditation. Since we are functioning in the world of form, it is seldom possible to jump straight into the void of spiritual sensing. If we retire to a quiet spot and begin directing our minds on the flow of contemplation of positive and truthful thoughts, the listening attitude begins to take over. Some find that it helps to read a few passages out of an inspiring book, some to read the Bible. Then when the mind is contemplating that which it is reading, the feeling of meditation can start. One can put down the book and go into a higher level, which is meditation. On the other hand, we can start by contemplating the rhythm of life, the blessings so freely presented by life, the love we experience. Though this is not prayer, it is the means to prayer. It is like the first commandment, or one part of the double thread.

Those who say that contemplation is purely mental and who think there is no place for it will never fulfill the act of prayer. On the other hand, those who never pass the contemplative stage do not arrive there either. When one has arrived in prayer, when one is living constantly in the listening attitude, aware of an inner guidance, there is no need for any techniques. As the Master said, "I live by the Father," or as Paul, "I live yet not I, but Christ [that state of consciousness] liveth in me." Until we are at that state we can only respond at the level we can comprehend. For some, getting down on their knees at bedside is the highest form they know; for others to humbly bow before a shrine is the way. None should be condemned. Every action with the right intent leads onward and upward.

Fasting

Jesus gave us another instruction to help us understand prayer and how it works. When we are faced with a particularly difficult problem, one that has not been met by listening, he tells us what to do. He said, "This one goes not out except by prayer and fasting."

Most people think that "to fast" is to abstain from food for a kind of spiritual purging. That is only man's limited interpretation. Any time we change a routine of thought or deed, we are fasting from the old. We have patterns of eating, working, recreation, and patterns of thought as well. Whenever we deliberately change the pattern for a while, we are fasting from our usual ways. The scientific principle behind the value of fasting is simple. One begins correcting an inharmonious activity by halting the activity until the fault is discovered. If one is being poisoned, it is wise to stop all eating until one discovers what is causing the ptomaine. Fasting stops man's ignorance so that truth can assert itself as the law of life. Fasting is giving up one's limited view of life so that Grace can show where mistakes are being made.

In the past few years it has become popular to go on "retreats." That is because people have become aware of the necessity to fast at times. The retreat is a fast from one's usual routine. Every time we sit down to pray, we are trying to fast from the errors of thought that have made us need to pray. Fasting is another way of fulfilling the commandment to love our neighbor for it is fasting from false judgment.

Another form of fasting is the fast from our own sense of personal responsibility. Whenever we turn to another and ask his help, we are fasting from our own ways. Through the centuries it has been found that some men have an awareness of prayer that can heal and break the bonds enslaving others. Jesus instructed his disciples that part of praying and fasting was also turning to each other for help. When we ask help of another, we desire to tune in to the other person's state of Grace for the moment. In the priesthood of all mankind there is no one who cannot at some time give help to another. You might be under the spell of ignorance at one time while some friend, no more spiritual than you, is not. At such a time the friend might well be able to see through the ignorance by which you are hypnotized, and lift you into freedom. At another time, you might be on the beam and the friend might have fallen for universal ignorance and you can help him. What each of you does is to love the other. You realize that for the moment your friend is possessed, but you realize that God is really the only power and you are judging righteously. You lift your friend into your vibration.

Vibration

Stripped of the occult mystery attached to such words as "spirit," "healing" or the "mystical," there is another explanation of the phenomenon of prayer that can be comprehended and understood even from the most materialistic of scientific reasoning. It is a supranatural explanation and may even be the best one for the new generation. Stretching to free ourselves from the cloak of past concepts of prayer, we can follow this explanation without in any way diminishing the mystery and beauty of the spirit.

This concept of prayer is based on an understanding of

vibration. As all matter is made up of atoms, the differences we behold in the material scene are made up of the differences of composition of the atoms, differences of density and assembly. Reduced to the state of unconditioned being, all is "atomness." The density or relationship of the atoms is seen as their vibration, and could we monitor that vibration we would hear a music, a music of the spheres, for music is vibration. Einstein revealed the secrets of the atom by revealing that all matter increased to the vibration or speed of light, became light itself. Just as the Master said, "I am the light," realizing his oneness with all being and cause.

The degree to which one descends into the world of matter is the degree of density down to the most solid of rocks and metals. One explanation given for the present occurrence of the appearance of flying saucers is that they have always been present, and that man has just now developed to the point where he can raise his level of vibration to tune into the level on which the saucers exist. On the days when one feels most free and lifted within, one feels less solid and heavy, less earthbound and weighted. On days when one indeed feels cut off and full of woe, one's arms and legs seem to weigh a thousand pounds each, every movement takes untold energy, and darkness dominates even midday.

It is at such times as this when we feel the need of help and reach out to others, cry out to God, lament our bondage. We recognize the arrival of help or freedom by the sense of release. Our vibration becomes more harmonious and loose. It is that same desire to find the freeing level of vibration beyond the solid, phenomenal world that induces man to reach out to drugs and drink instead of to God and neighbor. He really wants prayer, but has been tricked by the mind into thinking he can find its freeing love in a material substance.

Prayer is man's attempt to lift his vibration from the

density of matter into the same purity of spirit Jesus had when he said he was the "light." If man is really consciousness or spirit that has manifested a body, when he wants to change the body he must change the vibration or rhythm of life. A healing takes place when the vibration is changed from an inharmonious one to a harmonious one. In order to heal one must lift that vibration into harmony. The most striking example we have is that after Jesus' vibration of body was so violently interrupted at the crucifixion, in three days the vibration was altered and the body was restored.

Whenever, in the act of creating, the production has gone awry, when some error has crept in, it becomes necessary to disassemble the materials and again start listening within to catch the place where the wrong turn was made. Reducing the elements to their primal state and eliminating the errors is, again, tantamount to the commandment of the love of neighbor. This reduction to the basic vibration of life is the goal of prayer. When we counsel others to "take it easy," "relax," "get loose," "jelly," we are telling them to pray.

Let us take an example. For instance, one feels badgered, one feels a pressure, things are going wrong, nothing turns out right. Obviously the vibration is discordant. To plow right on blindly ahead only compounds the confusion. If one can stop and get one's feeling right, the whole situation will probably change. The first thing to do is to fast. Drop the problem for a moment. Go for a walk. Listen to some music. Even sleep can be a good thing at a time like that. Sleep is not necessarily escape, as many claim. It can be an inner desire to blank out the negative vibration in order to break through and make contact with harmony once more. At any rate, once a sense of release from the negative is felt, one can get a more truthful look at the situation that has been bothering one and have a much better chance to get into rhythm with it.

Gathering

Men have gathered in churches and groups because they sensed that there was some invisible truth in the prescript, "Where two or three are gathered together in my name, there am I." A lot of people thought Jesus meant his body would be there, not realizing that when he said "I" he meant his pure vibration, his invisible truth of being. That is why many became embittered with disappointment when they found nothing but a lot of human associations and a continuity of their human bondage. Observing from the level of the truth of being and the analysis of vibration, we uncover a truth that is not supernatural but highly natural.

Each individual has his mistaken knowledge of himself and life. Within him is also the truth of being that exists at a level beyond his ignorance. Whenever two or more are gathered together, they bring both their ignorance and their truth. The vibrations of their individual ignorances are many and individual. But the vibration of the truth of each individual is the same. When they gather together, ignorance remains individual but the truth is doubled over, is intensified. The vibration of truth is stronger than the individual ignorances, so it can pull the individuals into its vibrations. One can then leave freed, lifted, harmonious, and closer to the truth of one's being. Recognizing this effect, man has rightly acclaimed the merit of meeting together.

At the same time, many have been repulsed by meeting in groups. If the group vibration is not "in my name," in the name of truth, the effect can be the opposite of freedom. When a mob meets for the purpose of destruction, it can certainly confuse the innocent person who is at the meeting and fill him with negative fear or hate. If one goes into a night club that has a purely sensual or degrading vibration, it will leave one with that animal feeling if one stays there long enough. All of us have been places where we have said, "That place has a bad feeling," and we didn't want to be affected by it.

Though Jesus demonstrated this power of lifting the vibration, reestablishing wholeness, healing, and truth, none of his followers completely comprehended it until after he made the supreme demonstration. He told it in words and was not heard. He went so far as to take two of his most enlightened disciples to the mountain where he lifted his own vibration so high that he transfigured, the Mount of Transfiguration. He lifted his vibration into the most spiritual sense, and, still, it was beyond their comprehension.

When Jesus walked on the water and through the walls, he was revealing the possibility of lifting one's sense of being, one's vibration, to such a degree of light that materiality is no barrier. When Jesus healed broken bodies by lifting them into the vibration of harmony, he proved the power man has within his consciousness. When man comes to know that this same possibility is within himself, he will realize what Jesus meant when he said, "Verily, I say unto you, he that believeth on me, the works that I do shall he do also; and greater works than these shall he do."

CHAPTER 11

THE NOW AND THE HOW

Man has had it drummed into him for years about the efficacy of experiencing prayer. To be tantalized with the prospect of having a way to get free and yet having the technique withheld has been a bitter pill. Man says, "Okay, I'll buy that. I want to pray. But for God's sake give me something I can do. Give me some guidelines." This anguish gave rise in the past few years to what has been called the Metaphysical Movement. Christian Science, New Thought, Science of Mind, Unity, and the Church of Religious Science have all had one thing in common. They all believe that man now has the ability and understanding to lift prayer from its blind superstition into a conscious, scientific, consistent, understandable, and readily available reality.

Before a metaphysical technique of prayer can be explained, it is necessary to clear up the two places where man has made his greatest mistakes owing to his limited understanding. One is man's concept of time, the other is man's concept of matter or materiality.

Time

Time as we humanly conceive of it is not a reality. Only "now" exists. The past is over and does not exist. The future has not happened yet, and does not exist. Only "now" is. But man has not developed yet to the point where he is free of a belief in the time continuum; perhaps he will in the future. Man has developed a sense of three-dimensional sight which has freed him from the limited sense of sight a lot of the lower forms of life have. Most bugs, for instance, move around either by a kind of radar or by seeing only a flat world that is revealed by movement, not by the comprehension of depth. Until man develops the faculty to be freed of his finite sense of time, he must do so by an act of faith and understanding.

The reason this understanding is necessary is because the belief in time tricks man into most of his fear and sense of separation from God. When one is living in the "now" he is in a perfect state of poise. The minute one gets out of "now" troubles begin. Take a look. It is impossible to have a fear, care, or worry without projecting yourself out of this moment. You lament or feel guilt for something that happened in the past, you fear what will happen if you lose your job in the future, you fear getting sick in the future, getting old, being lonely. All fears require time to exist. All needs would not exist without time. Stop this second. You are reading. Where are your fears? When you start to think, the fears come back because your mind has taken your eyes off of the present moment and sent it forward or backward.

We only experience in the moment of "now." When we are out of "now," we do not experience life. We do not see that which is before our eyes. When we are thinking of the past or future, we miss the present and do not experience it wholly or fully. We are looking over the shoulder of life, so to speak. This rather existential desire to stay in "now" is why many of the Japanese do not clutter their homes with many objects of art, but, rather, put a single art work in a room so that it can be completely experienced. Then after a time they change the object and experience another in its place.

Many people find that large parties are unsatisfactory. They like meeting in small groups, but the crush of crowded gatherings disturbs them. The reason is that at large and transitory parties one scratches surfaces instead of making contact with others. The individuals are tempted out of "now" in that they are too busy looking beyond the person in front of them toward others they will be speaking with a little later. Ironically, when a guest gets to the next person he misses experiencing that one as well because he is already looking out of "now" to the next encounter.

Most of the accidents or discords we have are because we get out of the poise of "now." If we run and stumble and break our leg, it is because we are not watching what we are doing "now." Our mind is on the next appointment. If we had been in the "now" of running we would not have stumbled. Whenever we feel frustrated and pushed it is because our body is doing one thing and our mind is off in time. In such a state of frustration we burn the cake, spill the milk, flunk the exam, buy the wrong stock, or wreck the car. When we wreck the car, our being out of "now" may cost a life.

The closer we can live to the reality of this moment, the closer we are to living truthfully. Whenever a fear interrupts our life, we can nip it in the bud by recognizing that the situation has nothing to do with "now." We can stop and say, "What's that have to do with now? Nothing." And then we can reject it before it cheats us of our present fulfillment. Freed of dissipating our energies on a false sense of time, we can channel our whole selves into that which is taking place at this moment, and more quickly arrive at a harmonious and rewarding activity.

Living in "now" does not mean to refuse planning for the future. Ecclesiastes tells us, "To every thing there is a season, and a time to every purpose under heaven: a time to be born, and a time to die; a time to plant and a time to pluck up that which is planted." There comes a time when it is the proper moment to make a reservation, secure space, or plant seeds which will reach fruition months later. But to make reservations long before necessary out of fear or before preliminary elements are in place is not being in "now."

Whenever we feel we are starting to tighten up, grabbing hold of a feeling of tension or pressure, we know those conditions are a result of being out of "now." The tension is the signal for us to reject the ignorance and return to truth. The edict to "stay loose," or "get with it" is the instruction to get back in "now." By the same token, the desire to drink, or smoke marijuana, or use drugs may stem from the desire to have a feeling of "nowness." Those who use drugs are feeling tension and they believe narcotics will loosen them up and get them back into feeling the freedom of "now." The trick is that it seems temporarily to do so, only to push the users further out of "now" a bit later. When they learn why they want to use drugs they can then see why proper or really understood meditation or prayer will get them back in "now" and do the same thing only for real.

Those who call themselves existentialists have a sense of the all importance of "nowness," but many have again been fooled by their minds. They gorge, beyond any appetites, the human pleasures of life out of actual fear that they will not get enough of them in the future. That kind of existentialism has nothing to do with "now." In that way they are tricked out of "now" into self-abuse and debauchery.

When we are believing in time, and projecting "out of now," we are living under law in the Old Testament sense of life. We cannot judge another person or situation without leaving "now." We say, "That is bad," or "That is good," because of what it was in the past. We do not give it a chance to show what it is today. Our own egos are perpetuated purely and simply because we identify with the past. If we are living under law, then the past has some value for us because it shows us past mistakes. But the New Testament life of Grace shows us that each moment is new and infinitely different, each moment has a pure truth for itself alone.

To live in accord with the New Testament of life is to live each day at the highest possible pitch of integrity. One might think one's job is that of being a soldier, sailor, tinker, or tailor, but actually, under Grace, one's job is to live each moment in "now" to the highest level of one's consciousness. The form will take care of itself. This might lead one to be a soldier, sailor, tinker, or tailor, but the job is that of staying purely in "now."

Ends and Means

You can bisect the world, and know which people are living in "now" and which are not. The test cuts across all governments, institutions, professions, or activities. The test asks: Do they believe that the ends justify the means? If they do, they are not living in "now" and are not followers of Christ. Jesus said, "Take no thought for the morrow, what ye shall eat, or what ye shall drink." If you stay purely in "now," your tomorrow will be healthy and productive. As proof he went on to say, "Consider the lilies of the field, how they grow; they toil not, neither do they spin: and yet I say unto you, that even Solomon in all his glory was not arrayed like one of these."

There is no mystery behind the fact that the ends do not justify the means. All form and matter is the result of the recipe of life, of consciousness or imagination expressing itself in form. If we are close to the truth now, tomorrow's form will be the result. If we use lies and evil now, tomorrow's form will reflect this. When the Bible says, "God is not mocked," it could have said, "Truth is not mocked." There is nothing supernatural about it. You do it to yourself in terms of your "now."

It does not make any difference how nice a person is or how well he means. If he makes the mistake of believing that the ends justify the wrong kind of means, he reaps the result. After the second World War there was a resistance fighter in Sicily who became a modern Robin Hood. He stole from the rich with the admirable goal of feeding the poor. But that was the wrong means. Bit by bit he became conditioned by the means until he ended up being gunned down as a hardened killer and criminal. Perhaps he started out as a good man, but it made no difference, because his ignorance of the fact that the means conditions the ends turned him into a hunted criminal.

This same principle applies to nations as it does to people. In the first years of America, Thomas Jefferson said that every country should have a revolution every ten years. Every few years it is good to adjust to the present and shake off old habits and such. But this can be done democratically, without harming the individual, and with love. On the other hand, Karl Marx advocated change, but his followers took the path of using any means to get to the ends and in place of freedom they created bondage and tyranny.

Matter

This brings us to the second misunderstanding of which man now has to become clear before he can pray effectively—it is man's understanding of matter and being. Things exist for us only in terms of "nowness." We say they "are," "are being" now. In order to harmonize all things into a oneness and to really know them, we must be able to find some sense of "unconditioned being." Man sees everything in terms of form; so for him to sense unconditioned being without form is as hard as it is for him to think without using time.

As all matter is made up of atoms, where we start to judge is in our interpretation of the qualities the different objects have. Then we start to say, "That one with those qualities is good, and that one with those qualities is bad." To get really free, to be able to have the experience of prayer, it is necessary to be able to feel or sense the pure "beingness" or "isness" of things and people. Unconditioned being is pure "isness." It is the admission that something does exist, and that it can be seen without being judged. It just "is"—not bad or good. Those who are attracted to existentialism are attracted for the main reason that it advocates staying in "now" and does not judge, that it concentrates just on "being," on "beingness." In that respect, Jesus was the greatest existentialist known to man. His "beingness" was so strong that it is still here and alive today.

The truth of being is that God, as the ultimate cause of all, is appearing as everything that is seen. Matter is spirit (isness) formed. First God being "is," and then God appearing "as"; as tree, as cat, as person, as house, as all . . . This is another way of saying that consciousness is appearing as form. If one has some "feel" of "now," "is," and "as," one can do the two things that are necessary for the experience of prayer.

To Impersonalize

In order to experience effective prayer, we must do two things, two deliberate and definite things: we must "impersonalize" and "nothingize." These are the same two things that Jesus told us to do. To love our neighbor we must impersonalize him, and to love God we must make all powers nothing, apart from the one power of God.

The first law of spiritual nature is that we must never deal with our concept of person, thing, or condition in the external world but must go within and there know the truth about person or thing. Man is only an instrument through which ignorance operates while it has power over him. As man did not invent integrity, honesty, or any of the qualities man expresses, we cannot either blame him when he expresses the opposite nor praise him when he expresses the virtues. When man is being dominated by either one, we are dealing not with the man but the condition.

When we sit down to pray in order to get a release from anger or concern over that which someone has done to us or to another, we must deliberately release that individual from responsibility. We can judge the deed, but not the living person. This is what it means by "love your enemies." It does not mean that to love our enemies we are supposed to let them walk all over us, or that we should love their ignorant behavior. That is the kind of mistake that has frustrated many a person who has instinctively wanted to love. To try to approve of your neighbor's stupid actions is saying that evil is good. But, you do love your neighbor when you realize that he is trapped by his ignorance, that he is soul possessed for the moment. Your neighbor does not want to be stupid, no one wants to poison himself. If he knew better, he would not do whatever he is doing wrongly. To realize this about your neighbor is to "impersonalize" and release him.

Most people love children; that is, they do not harshly judge a small child when he makes mistakes for which a grownup might be severely judged. They try to enlighten the child or they remove themselves or some object in order for the mistake not to happen again, but they do not judge the child himself. Therefore, when there is someone whom you cannot keep from judging, it is wise to follow the Master's instruction to "go and make peace," go and impersonalize the conduct of that person. But thereafter it would be wise to remove yourself as much as possible from the person to keep from being tempted again. At any rate, there is no excuse for blaming anyone. When you openly blame anyone it only makes him feel more guilty. As causing guilt is the opposite of loving, it means you are hating, not loving. When you realize that the same Grace that operates for all living beings is operating for him as well as for yourself, you can release him. When you have impersonalized him, yourself, and the problem and have seen it as part of universal hypnotism, you are ready for the next step which will bring you to the experience of prayer.

To Nothingize

To know the nothingness of error is the rudder that guides the ship of life. It is the fulfillment of the commandment of the love of God. God is the only power. God is all. When we know that, we are loving God. The act of impersonalization is the act of knowing "what is not"; therefore, when we know the nothingness of powers apart from God we are knowing "what is."

There is truth, there is God, but there is no God "and." God is "allness." Everything we see that appears to be apart from God is an illusion. To "overcome the world" is to cease from resisting the appearances of evil. Human sense claims that there are powers apart from God; therefore we overcome the world when we "nothingize" those beliefs within ourselves. When we have ceased resisting evil or judging it, we have surrendered to the one power. To "nothingize" is to surrender to God. There is nothing to fight, nothing to resist, nothing to overcome.

When we sit down to pray because we believe there is a power of evil that can make us lose our jobs, when we sit down to pray because we believe in a power of loneliness that can keep us from peace, we must immediately realize the "nothingness" of those powers. We do not try to talk ourselves out of the power that we are accepting because that is resisting it and only increases its hold on us. Instead we "nothingize" it by knowing "what is." There is nothing that can harm a person who knows only one power, one cause, one being, one life, one self.

Prayer is a complete circle. It is the circle of life or spirit: to be spiritual is to be free, to be free is to be unbound, to be unbound is to impersonalize, to impersonalize is to live in "now," to live in "now" is to have no judgment, to have no judgment is to realize there is no power but God's, to realize there is no power but God's is to "nothingize," to "nothingize" is to be released, is to be spiritual, and we are back where we started. The circle is closed.

CHAPTER 12

A MATTER OF
LIFE AND DEATH

All the talk about the double aspect of life, about the "without" and the "within," about the necessity of comprehending that we are both "men of earth, and men of God" is only window dressing. We must understand this double thread of our life, and we must urgently hang on to an awareness of each side in order to have a rich full life. But everything is for nothing if we are not alive.

Take an automobile, for instance. It has its visible body carefully designed, painted, and engineered. It also has the invisible motor that is the power behind the machine—the without and the within. But if the third element, the gasoline, is missing, the car is useless. It seems amazing that something as ephemeral as gasoline should make that difference. To further complicate matters, it might take many months to fashion the automobile's body and motor, but once they are built they can last a lifetime with only minor repairs; however, the fuel runs out daily and must be replenished daily. Without a source to go to, without a knowledge of what the fuel is and where to put it, the desire to live, the time spent building the machine, and the shiny automobile itself all are for nothing. An automobile without the essence of life is a dead automobile.

The Christian message says, "The last enemy that shall be destroyed is death." In order to call oneself a Christian one must know first what death is, what causes it, and how to overcome it.

What Death Is

What man calls death is an illusion. When a seed falls into the ground and breaks open, it appears to die, but that death is actually only the movement of life from one form into another. It is not death. Only by appearing to die and break open does a tree grow from the seed. When a fire appears to kill the burning wood it is only releasing the substance of the wood into another form of energy. This form of death is the creative necessity; without it there can be no movement of life, no growth. That is why Jesus said, "Verily, verily, I say unto you, except a corn of wheat fall into the ground and die it abideth alone: but if it die, it bringeth forth much fruit."

A few verses later we are told that there is another kind of death, a true death, that we must learn to avoid in order to have eternal life. "I am the vine, ye are the branches. He that abideth in me, and I in him, the same bringeth forth much fruit: for without me ye can do nothing. If a man abideth not in me, he is cast forth as a branch, and is withered." The "I" he is talking about is the source of his being, and that source of his being is the same source of everyone's being. That is why he could say that he was within us, we within him, and God within all things. To die is to be cut off from the source of life. To be fully alive is to be fully in tune with the source of life.

What Causes Death

When we know what death is, we take a look at what causes death. Any ignorance that causes us to believe we have a life apart from God cuts us off. As ignorant individuals we believe we have a life of our own disconnected and separate from all other life. Without losing sight of the fact that we do indeed have individuality, let us take a look at what makes us live. Has any one of us ever made a heart beat, a piece of food digest itself, a gland secrete, an eye see, or an ear hear? No. *Life lives us.* We do not live life. We have no life of our own. We are powerless to live. It not only lives us, *it is us.* The belief that we have a life of our own is an illusion. This thing that renews the cells in our body, that makes the complicated body machinery grow, that operates the brain, that supplies talent and ability is the truth of us. Whenever we think we can take some credit for these operations, or that they are some kind of personal possession that we, in our ego sense, can control, we are ignorant of our true selves.

We are also ignorant of ourselves when we consciously or subconsciously think we are our bodies alone. It has been said that every cell in our bodies regenerates itself every seven years. If that is the case, there is not a cell of you that was here seven years ago. Yet, if you are five times seven years old you do not say, "I, number five, say hello," when someone greets you. You have a body, but you are not body alone. You are that which lives that body, that renews it year after year. Your "I" is the source of life.

It is impossible to understand that one is actually that which lives the body or to apply this belief to oneself without the strength to double think. This is not saying that a "you" does not exist, a "you" that possesses a body, talent, individuality, and a you that is even deserving of

credit. When you are functioning without ignorance, you
are expressing pure God, and it is right that both you and
the world recognize it. We are like waves in the ocean. A
wave is one with the whole ocean, yet it is individual in its
size and shape. As the wave has its being from the ocean,
it contains all of the ocean within it, all of it. If waves
could glory, a wave could glory in the fact that it was one
with the whole ocean. If it wanted to take individual
credit, it would be wrong. That is why Jesus slapped his
disciples with his words when they were bragging about
their individual miracles. He said, "Rejoice only that your
names are writ in heaven." Whenever we either take personal credit for talents and virtues OR deny that we personally express talents and virtues, we are cutting ourselves off, and, like a wave that is cut off from the ocean,
we die as we dry up.

We have seen that the cause of death is action based on
ignorance. These ignorant actions separate us from the
source; so before proceeding to the final step of how we
overcome ignorance we must clear up the ignorance attached to six words that have most often tricked man into
a sense of separation from God. Consciously tying the
double thread of life together by realizing there is a validity
in the accepted concept of these words, we must at the
same time see another meaning for them. The words are
selfishness, humility, sin, morality, loneliness, and denial.

Selfishness is considered a bad thing by society. We are
told we must not be selfish. Yet every action man
performs has a selfish desire motivating it. He is hungry;
so he goes to the refrigerator. He has the need to create;
so he paints a picture. Even Schweitzer found that he
could only fulfill his "selfish" need to help his fellow man
by going to the African jungles to administer to the na-
tives. Whenever we reach out to God, it is because of a
self-need. This is good. Without such selfish needs man

would sit like a log, never moving. Every action, no matter how small, has self behind it.

We have God within us; so our first responsibility is to ourselves. We must keep ourselves open, healthy, and strong; then we can help others. If we pull ourselves down, and are tricked into thinking that we should make ourselves overexhausted for others, we end up by not only harming ourselves but also being of no help to others. That is why Jesus retreated to the mountaintop to get himself restored at times. There were still people in the world needing to be healed and fed, but he knew that unless he kept his contact with his source he could be of no help to anyone. When he was restored and strong, he returned and continued his ministry of healing and feeding the masses. Whenever any of us, mothers or others, are tricked into believing that we should break our health and strength by taking too much care of our families' needs, we end up doing them more harm than good. We should be spiritually selfish. We should first and foremost keep ourselves in spiritual and physical health and second, use that strength to help others. We have God-given talents, and we must selfishly protect and channel those talents creatively.

Humility is often seen as an act of debasing oneself, as the opposite of selfishness. But to debase oneself, to punish oneself, to degrade oneself in any way is the opposite of true humility. To refuse to act because one fears one might do something wrong is also to reject true humility. We have a responsibility to remember we are one with the ocean, the source, and whenever we act with the dignity of that realization, we are acting with humility. When we recognize that God is the source of our life and talent, we are responding with humility. True humility is the pure realization that "I live, yet not I," that God is the truth of my being. Having the courage to follow your inner voice, to recognize you have that within you which will lead you, is true humility.

Sin is the acceptance of any ignorance. Whenever we accept a false sense of ourselves we are sinning. Whatever tricks us into cutting ourselves off is a sin. Oddly enough, most often what we call sin is really only a distortion of a virtue. Of course, that very distortion is what makes it a sin. The greater the virtue, the greater the sin; the lesser the virtue, the smaller the sin. For example, it is considered a virtue for man to be creative, but when man tries to fulfill that virtue by stealing from other people's creations it is a sin. It is a virtue to experience the joy of being in "now," but alcohol and drugs induce an artificial feeling of contact with God, so that those who use them for that purpose are distorting the virtue. The supreme sin of all is for one to take one's own life, yet the supreme virtue of all is to do as Jesus said and die to our false sense of self in order to have life eternal.

Immorality and sin are actually the same thing. Any ignorant act is an immoral one. As spiritual man does not live under law, what may be immoral for one person may not be for another. What may be considered immoral for one generation may not be for another. Whatever makes people feel cut off or guilty is immoral for them. The rigid puritanical society under which many Americans lived a couple of generations ago considered it sinful to play cards or visit motion pictures on Sunday, and those who lived under those laws felt guilty when they violated them. If going to a movie made them feel guilty, it was indeed immoral for them because anything that made them feel guilty and cut off from God was immoral.

It may shock some to hear this, but the test we can make to determine whether or not an act might be immoral for us individually is to ask ourselves if the act would make us feel guilty. If there is really no cause for guilt in the action, then it is probably not an immoral act for the individual. At first this kind of rule sounds like a license for all kinds of liberty, but it is not.

There are spiritual truths governing man's respect for his own body, and his respect for his fellow man. A violation of these truths produces guilt in even the most hardened or mesmerized person. When we say that nothing is immoral which does not make us feel guilty, we are assuming the double-thinking aspect that the person has the capacity to face guilt. We learn that the body is "the temple of the living God." So to disrespect the body is an immoral act. In that light, gluttony should make people feel guilt and show them that they are performing an immoral act by eating too much. Anything that is not harmful to self or neighbor is most likely not an act of immorality. Anything that does not cause us to hate ourselves or feel cut off from God, from right, and from good in one way or another could be considered moral. We have only to turn within, to "listen," and we can know.

It remains to consider the last two conditions that we have said the world sees out of focus—denial and loneliness. Denial is considered a bad act in betraying another person or cutting oneself off from another person. But actually denial is often necessary for fulfillment—fulfillment of both people. When the disciples denied Jesus, it made it possible for them to find the Christ within themselves. They could then no longer lean on Jesus as a person and were forced to find their own contact with God. On the other hand, by being denied Jesus went on to fulfill himself and demonstrate fully that he had God within him.

It seems like a contradiction, but the better the parent or teacher, the more difficult it is to break away and become whole. When a teacher, for example, is accomplished at his task it is harder for the student to get free, but break away he must in time. If the student does not break away, he will never be equal to the teacher, he will never find that he has a teacher right inside himself. That is why we are told in the New Testament that when we are young we have nurses and tutors, but when we are older we take our place as "heir, and joint heir with Christ, in God." An heir does not mean "inferior to," but rather, "of the same potential." Only by what looks like denial, when we doubt and question, do we receive the answers. Often we must lose faith in order to find true faith, and to find that we too have the ability to personally know God.

There is a day when it is time for a child to find the Father that is within himself. When that day arrives, it signals that the child is approaching manhood and wholeness. Conflicts seem to rise between the parent and child. This works from both sides. The parent finds more fault with the young, and the young with the parent. This is a creative necessity for both the parent and the child. The child needs it to push him out of the nest so that he will go and become creative and whole—and the parent needs it because his creative job with the child is over. He must now turn his own energies to other things. To hang on to the relationship at the old level of parent and child does no one any good. To realize this changes the relationship into a creative sharing of adults and gives freedom and joy to all. When Jesus said, in Luke 14:16, "If any man come to me, and hate not his father, and mother, and wife, and children, and brethren, and sisters, yea, and his own life also, he cannot be my disciple," he did not mean it was necessary to lose a sense of love. He meant there comes a time when one must lean only on the truth within one's own Christhood.

Loneliness is the reason it is hard for one deliberately to step out on one's own. The greatest fear man has is the fear of loneliness. Beyond his fear of lack, sickness, or physical death is the fear of loneliness. When man is alone he is tempted to feel cut off from life. As long as there is another person he feels he has a bridge to the rest of life and mankind. Most people get married not because of sex, but because they do not want to be alone.

There is a great deal of difference between loneliness and the experience of aloneness. To be completely one's self everyone must, at one time or another, experience the state of aloneness. When one is alone there are no outside vibrations from others affecting them, no combinations of consciousness at work. One's life then is purely a product of one's own individual consciousness. The value of this experience is that only after experiencing aloneness can we truly know who we are. Only through aloneness can we purely experience our individual link with God. After the experience, or after renewing the experience, we can then go forth and be a better mate or partner because we know who we are and what we have to offer. When we no longer find the need to lean on anything, we experience spiritual aloneness. In this kind of aloneness is our allness.

The Overcoming

After knowing what death is, and the conditions that cause it, we find that Jesus tells us in the Book of Matthew how we can overcome it. He said that we can blaspheme or sin against the son and be forgiven, but if we blaspheme or sin against the Holy Spirit it is the unforgivable sin, the sin unto death. We have already learned that we are sinning against our neighbor or the visible son whenever we judge by appearances. We have learned that we sin against God whenever we accept or resist evil as a power apart from God. These we can do and get over it, but when we sin against the Holy Spirit we cut ourselves off and die.

The Holy Spirit is like the gasoline in the tank of your life. It is the life force that makes everything happen. It is a happening. It is the act of experiencing. To be ignorant of the Holy Spirit is to be ignorant of your true self, and when you are ignorant of yourself you are cut off from the source. When you are ignorant of your neighbor or of God, you are not fulfilling the two commandments of love, and when you are ignorant of yourself you are not loving yourself. When you do not love yourself, you are sinning against the Holy Spirit.

If God is the truth of our being, if God is all there is, then to know ourselves is to know God. To love ourselves is to know we are one with God. Then we see God's life as our very own life. The mind reels before this revelation because the implication is obviously "He is saying, I am God." That is true. We cannot have it both ways. If we accept God as being allness, then there cannot be God and us. The unqualified total realization of this caused Jesus to say, "I and the Father are one," "If ye see me, ye see the Father." Right away we want to say, "Maybe that was true about Jesus, but it isn't true about me." But Jesus said, over and over, that everything that was true of him was true of all mankind, and if one cannot accept Jesus' words when he said "I am in my Father, and ye in me, and I in you," one should ask oneself why and how one can call oneself a Christian.

This has to be comprehended in the light of all that has gone before. Certainly no one is saying that hypnotized man who believes that he is cut off from God and must live under law is like Christ. But when we have died to that false sense of self, there is nothing left but God. And we can die to that sense if we follow the instructions we were given by the Master, if we stop judging man and if we know God, if we know our oneness with all of life.

When we realize that all mankind shares the same source of life that we do, we realize that whenever we harm another we are harming ourselves—our very own self. If the world actually realized this, doing "unto others as you would have them do unto you" would not be considered a noble act but, rather, a most practical act of self-preservation. It would realize that any other act is a sin against the Holy Spirit that causes death. Take, for instance, the electric current in the source of power for all the outlets in a house. If someone sticks a screwdriver into one socket and blows that socket out, he not only blows that one out but all the lights on the circuit as well. We are all hooked up with all of mankind, and whenever we harm another we are harming ourselves. War, for no matter what reasons, is the great sin against self and the Holy Spirit. Whenever a gun is fired, it is self firing at self. War is the greatest antithesis to love of self.

Our bodies are only a part of all other bodies. In an attempt to get free from our sense of separation and to see our actual oneness with all we behold, we might take the example of the television set. When the set is turned off it is dead, worthless, and not television. Only when it is alive and there is a picture on the screen is it television, and this picture is shared with all other sets that tune in. The content, whether destruction or beauty, and the set are one. In this respect, as humans, we are a part of everything we behold. We are our neighbors, our family, our world. Every leaf on a branch, every branch of the tree are all fed from the same life. If I war against the other leaves or branches, I am warring against my own source of life. I am not loving my self.

Whenever I think badness is bad, or goodness is good, whenever I think some are inferior and some superior, whenever I judge life in any way that is not loving—I am sinning against life itself and myself. On the other hand, my conscious oneness with God constitutes my oneness with all being. I love God when this "I," the "I" that is at the center of me, is behind my actions. In the world of mankind there are many names, but there is really one name that fits them all, that is "I." The name of God is "I." God himself told Moses, "I AM THAT I AM. . . . Thus shalt thou say unto the children of Israel, I AM hath sent me unto you." When we realize that that is our name, we are loving our self, we are loving the Holy Spirit, and we are experiencing life.

CHAPTER 13

THE TRIUNE WAY

❧

The realization that there were three distinct aspects, body, mind, and spirit, which made up the whole man gave rise to the importance of the Trinity as the foundation of the Christian message. Reconciling the three aspects into oneness, into the Trinity, is the basis for all of life and creativity. There is nothing vague or occult about it. No creation of any kind, in science, art, or business, takes place properly without the balance of these three in one. Our success as a creator or a person is when we attain the Trinity, the triune life.

When we have found the nature of ignorance, faced the apparent limitations, broken down the appearance into its parts, impersonalized the faults, and given up making human judgments—we have fulfilled the commandment of the love of neighbor. This love of the Son is one corner of the Trinity.

When we have lifted our consciousness into that which we know is the truth of life, the nature of all truth; when we have remembered that the only power is truth and that all other negative appearances get their power only by a distortion of the one power—we have "nothingized" and fulfilled the commandment of the love of God. That is another corner of the foundation of the Trinity.

The one thing missing now, the last aspect, is the Holy Spirit. The Holy Spirit is more ephemeral than the other two for it is not a thing—it is an experience. It is the experience of life itself. That is why you can sin against the other two without death, but when you deny life itself, when you deny the spirit of life within your self, all else is of no avail. Without the experience, without the miracle, all else is mental, all else is limited to nothing but human knowledge.

The Trinity is so difficult to comprehend because it is in itself a kind of double thinking that is always necessary for life. The secret behind the Pyramids is an example of this. From the ground, one can see two sides of a pyramid at a time. One can walk around the whole pyramid and see all sides at one time or another, but never all at once. It requires an act of faith, a double thinking. Never can man of earth see all sides from his finite position. Only if man can view the pyramid from above, only while standing on the very pinnacle, the pinnacle of Spirit, can man view the whole at once—then he is no longer viewing it as man of earth.

To understand the effect of mind on body one must, for a moment, stop seeing spiritually. To know the effects of spirit on body, one must, for a moment, transcend the logical mind. To understand the relationship of mind and spirit, one must transcend the body and be able to comprehend how consciousness manifests itself in form. The three sides can never be seen at the same split second. They can be experienced when one has experienced the wholeness in meditation or prayer, and only when one reaches that selfless state.

That is where "free will" comes in. In the Christian following we are taught that man has free will. Most people in the East accept fatalistically that there is no free will. Both are right. At the level of the invisible there is a changing and conditioning that is beyond the will of man. Even on the human plane, man may seem to be able to choose his actions, but actually all his experiences in life have added up to condition his responses. If God is the only power, then man's free will can have no real power. This side is beyond man's comprehension. In human life it is important that man believes that he has free will—and he does.

Man has the will to remember. Every time he makes a decision he can remember. He can listen. He can return to the highest truth he knows. This remembrance will activate his imagination, and the forms of his life will reflect his remembering. Man can choose to remember, he can choose to listen. We have the free will to be or not to be like Jesus Christ because we have seen his example and we can remember.—A man's integrity is the degree of will he exerts in remembering.—We can have the will to remember to pray, to remember to listen, to remember not to judge, to remember when pressure comes that we are out of "now," and through this remembering we can experience the Holy Spirit.

That is the experience of prayer. At that moment the Trinity is one, three in one, three *as* one. It is matter. It is spirit. It is perfection. It is imperfection. It is truth. It is illusion. It is man. It is God. No part is left out.

The Trinity is ever present. It can be seen in infinite manifestation. Out of the past (one corner) and the future (the other corner) comes the experience of "now." Out of material and spiritual comes the experience of balance and equilibrium. Out of the Old Testament pre-Christian comes the New Testament Christian, and the result is the whole man. This Christian is a trinity because he is made up of three sides: One side is God, the Father—"isness." One side is God the Son—God "as." One side is God the

Holy Spirit—"I," the spirit or experience that takes place within the man.

The vision of "I," oneness, the kingdom, the Trinity, is the opposite of guilt and puts aside the world of hypnotism and law. The "I" in the midst of me feeds me, clothes me, houses me. "I" provides everything necessary. This "I" is the spiritual son, "I" am the invisible presence, "I" am the spirit of God, and to sin against the "I" is to sin unto all death, for "I" am both father and son. "I" am all.

The Trinity is oneness. "I" is one. It is "I the father," "I the son," "I the Holy Spirit,"—"I." The method is love. The example is no more plainly given to us than in the thirteenth chapter of I Corinthians. "Though I speak with the tongues of men and angels, and have not love [truth, judgeless truth] I am become as sounding brass or a tinkling symbol. And though I have the gift of prophecy, and understand all mysteries, and all knowledge: and though I have all faith, so that I could remove mountains, and have not love, I am nothing."

We struggle for the gift of prophecy, the gift of being able to interpret the truths in the Bible, the gift of being able to sit down and tell others metaphysical truths and reveal knowledge. Though we have all wisdom catalogued in our brain; though we have the conviction of faith in that wisdom; though we have proved we can move mountains and split the atom—we are nothing if we do not have the experience which is Love.

"And though I bestow all my goods to feed the poor" —though we leave no stone unturned in trying to be good by giving away our goods to feed the poor; "and though I give my body to be burned"—though we will even let ourselves be crucified; "and have not love, it profiteth me nothing." Though we allow all the things the world under law calls virtue, it profits us nothing.

"Love suffereth long, and is kind: love envieth not; love vaunteth not itself, is not puffed up." It takes a lot of

human frustration not to judge; it keeps one humble and
unpuffed up. "Love doth not behave itself unseemly, seek-
eth not her own, is not easily provoked, thinketh no evil;
rejoiceth not in iniquity, but rejoiceth in truth." As Love
is truth, it rejoiceth only in its self, in the pure awareness
of life and oneness.

"Love never faileth. But whether there be prophecies,
they shall fail; whether there be tongues, they shall cease;
whether there be knowledge, it shall vanish away." For all
the prophesying, all the teaching, all the knowledge,
really does not mean a thing. How many times we see a
truth and vow never to forget it, only to see it vanish away
in a day's or a week's time. Words dry up and lose their
strength, and if we cling to them we cling to a broken
reed.

"For we know in part, and we prophesy in part. But
when that which is perfect is come, then that which is in
part shall be done away." When we know the laws of
human life, when we find individual truths, we know only
the parts; we know only imperfect truth. But when the
whole comes, we know perfection and the limitations of
the parts are done away with. We can talk truths, but
when we see the Source of Truth, Perfect Being, we come
to the realization or experience for one second of Pure
Being, God, Pure God. Then the parts fall away. If we
experience God, then the parts will take care of themselves. When the vessel of our being is full of the one
being, there is no room left for anything else—no space
for error, or for ignorance. When we concern ourselves
with the parts, we never arrive at the fullness, but when
we attain the fullness we fulfill all the parts.

"When I was a child, I spake as a child, I understood as
a child, I thought as a child: but when I became a man
[when I became the whole man, the Trinity] I put away
childish things." When I had to pray to a God apart from
myself, when I had to discipline myself, put myself in
school as a child, I was a child. But when I became a man

and realized that I was heir and joint heir with Christ in God, I put away childish thoughts and became a MAN.

"For now we see through a glass darkly, but then [when I am a man] face to face: now I know in part; but then shall I know even as also I am known." We are half in school and half out of school. We are still knowing in part. None of us is completely graduated, just as Jesus was not complete until the final end; but just as the truth of us is revealed, we will be that truth, wholly, Holy.

"And now abideth faith, hope, love, these three; but the greatest of these is love." The Trinity: Faith in the Sonship, Hope in the guidance of the Father consciousness, one principle, one power, and the experience itself. Faith, hope, and love, but the greatest is love, for faith and hope mean nothing without love.

Whatever way we come to this experience is prayer. As prayer is not under the law of man, there is no formula that applies to all mankind. No prayer really begins until man each time arrives at the realization that there is no way he, through himself, can pray. Each time there is a moment of giving up, a moment of helplessness. Unless he feels that moment of helplessness, unless he feels he has lost the ability to pray, he is doing it mentally and no experience of the Holy Spirit will take place. Each time man creates a work of art he experiences that same moment of helplessness before creativity within begins to pour forth into his consciousness. Each act of creating is an act of prayer. Schools can give us the tools of creation, the commandments, but the creation must take place anew each time. Man must be reborn each time.

The following example is not a formula but only an example of one man's journey from the world of his daily life into the eternal city of God:

In the beginning, I am faced with a personal problem, a lack. The first step is to impersonalize it. I didn't invent it. Then why do I have it? Because I am heir to a degree of a sense of separation from God; I am heir to a degree of ignorance. This ignorance is universal. I didn't invent it. It isn't my fault. It is there. That I'll admit. I am trying to pray because I feel the need to free myself from the problem. I want to return to my father's house. I want to loosen the tension I feel—the pull, the heaviness. I can only get rid of it first by realizing and then by experiencing Truth. Realization comes only as an act of Grace. I cannot earn it. If I try to earn Grace, then it is not a gift and the Scriptures tell me that Grace is a gift of God. A gift of God. If prayer will work only to the degree that I am fulfilling the law of right and wrong, then there can be no prayer, but only, instead, the law of retribution.

My problem is not a personal one, but a universal one— the belief in separation from need. Is it a problem of supply, of health, of lack? No, the problem is my belief that I am out, off from my good. Problems are like actors in a stock company: they wear a different mask each week, but the actor is the same. The actor is the sense of separation from God. The problem has nothing to do with something out there. For myself, it is not a problem with my family relationship. It is not a problem with my neighbor—it only wears that mask.

So the first thing I must do is to let myself off the hook, release my sense of personal responsibility. But I must also release my neighbor. If he is acting under the influence of ignorance and pettiness, it signifies only that he too is operating under the spell of ignorance, that he is being used by ignorance, that he is soul possessed by ignorance for that moment. But it is not his fault, any more than it was man's fault when he believed the world was flat. I must not try to bring God down to the level of my ignorance, of my neighbor; rather, I must hold my neighbor up to the light of truth. One day he too will be free. I must now drop him from my thought by releasing him. I must impersonalize him. Now I have loved my neighbor, I have loved my enemy, for I have relinquished judgment. I have renounced judgment of myself as well.

I have not yet released God. I keep expecting God to do something for me. By that expectation I am believing that God is withholding something from me. I am believing that there is an evil power operating in my life about which God needs to know. When I resist evil, I give it power, and it shows that the belief exists within me. I am not using my free will to remember what I know about God, truth, and life. I must free God from my personal desire and limitation. I am no longer bowing down before false idols, false powers. I release God by knowing the truth about God. Before, I was fulfilling the love of neighbor by releasing him; now I must love God by knowing what really does exist.

There is only one Being, one "isness," one infinite cause and truth. That is God, omnipresent, omniscient. Anything that testifies otherwise is the dream of ignorance to which man is subject. Limitation does not exist; it is only an image of the mind, an appearance. But the truth is the kingdom of God, eternal life and harmony, and it is within me. I don't have to find it. It is. My only need is to become aware of it and its "isness," to realize that it already is. God was the beginning, and all that was made was made by God. Anything that God did not make does not exist. God is love, and as God is infinite, there is nothing else. There is only one God, and the I in the midst of me is that God. There is no power besides the I that I am. That I that I am is immortal and eternal. In my oneness with that God, all intelligence, all wisdom, all life, and all spirit is embodied within me.

"Speak father, thy servant heareth." And it says, "It is my good pleasure to give you the Kingdom. Son, I am ever with thee." It seems to lead me from the sense of self into the sense of Beingness. "Be not afraid. It is I."

Even within the so-called sin, I am. If I make my bed in Hell, I am there. There is no place you can go that I am not, not even in the illusion of worldly cares and worldly problems. If there were worldly problems, even if there were the illusion and Me, there would be two, but even where the illusion and ignorance are, I am, so there is only one when the eyes of truth are open.

If you sin, I am in that sin leading you to me, and when you awake, you will find that there never has been even a sin, for I am all there is. You have no responsibility—nothing. Emptiness. Release. Let go. Rest in me. Rest. Rest from the words. Rest from struggling. Stop. Give up. Believe that I am here. I have always been here and now. The veil will be lifted from the cradle, and we find that I am a babe inside of your very own being, in the center of you. And instead of being a helpless babe, I am really your strength. In fact, I am all that is. Everything that has pushed you forward to this spot has been me, for I am your life. The pains, the worries, the fears—all of these have only been masks to hide me from the world until I was ready.

No fear. No struggle. I am resting in the everlasting arms. This I is the only being that is born this moment. It is the only truth of my existence. This I is in every man. This I is in my neighbor, and in my family. When I return to the level of man, if I expect to see changes, if I expect to see new forms of human perfection, I am denying that I now exist. To feel the world needs healing, to feel the world need teaching, to feel the world needs to find new truths—is denying that I am the truth, the way and the life eternal. No need. No need.

"Rejoice only that your name is writ in heaven." Do not rejoice that you can manipulate the human scene. Rejoice that you have treasures stored up that moth and rust cannot destroy. Rejoice that you have human identity to hide behind; rejoice that you can walk through life with a smile. Rejoice because you can look in the eyes of others and know that the same secret is the truth of them. Rejoice that you may stumble and fall once more as a human because you are both human and God.

"I have come that ye might be fulfilled" . . . fulfilled. And now we find that the Kingdom has always been here, that I have been with you since before Abraham was. And now we know what the Robe is. Always we thought that the Robe would come from without us to clothe and protect us, that we would find external truths to protect us. But now we know that the Robe is within us; that it is the truth of our being. With the cloak of our humanity stripped off we stand protected, maintained, sustained in the Robe of the I that I am. The Robe is our protection, our love, our fulfillment, our Being, our Oneness, our ALL. Rest.

Then prayer was complete. The words, as such, are of no value. They can be of value only as they show that the experience, the Holy Spirit, occurred in the consciousness of a man. A beautiful painting is not the miracle; it is the result of the miracle of creation that the artist experienced. But if great art can inspire us to attain that miracle, and that is what it does, then it has served a purpose. It has returned man to his beginning point as consciousness, not form.

The map has served its purpose. The trip is complete. Genesis started with the creation of the universe and the last chapters of Revelation announce the same creative principles. "I am the Alpha and the Omega, the beginning and the end, the first and the last. Blessed are they that do his commandments, that they may have right to the tree of life, and may enter in through the gates into the city."

CHAPTER 14

THE CUP OF LIFE

At best, man is shown only the tiniest moments of the experience of the absolute, but from those moments come his greatest fruits. Those who try to induce the experience of the absolute by material means may find some kind of distorted sensual experience, but these experiences seldom if ever bring creative results at the material level. Yet the mystery of a valid moment of prayer, a valid mystical experience, is that it always results in a better life for mankind, greater art, or greater spiritual truth manifest in the consciousness of man to free man.

The mystical excesses of the seekers both of the West and of the East have developed various kinds of emotional orgies and even a mental imbalance that has mistakenly been called mysticism or religious experience. Those who have rolled on the ground in catatonic fits, or envisaged weird uninterpretable signs have produced no fruits of value, and by their fruits men are always known.

Others have propounded complicated systems of brain-washing that induce their followers to reject life, to turn from the adventure of living, and to escape into a dream world. But life has been given to us for a purpose. In all its agony and ecstasy, life is a glorious adventure. When we are no longer trying to escape, we can look at life, find its rhythm, and experience it fully. Only by experiencing all the misery and joy of being a human, and by the exquisite moments of identifying with the infinite beyond, do we live life fully.

We look out the window and we behold a tree. We delight in its beauty and its shade. To us that tree has no intelligence or emotion, but if it did we would see that its life is one constant round of problems for the tree. The sun comes up in the morning and there is a problem of what to do with the heat that brings on expansion; so the tree draws its sap from the roots to take care of it. At night another problem faces the tree. What shall it do with the sap, now that the temperature has dropped and its surface is shrinking? It then pushes the sap down into the roots. And the constant daily round of problems continues. From our deified point of view, what are constant problems to the tree are only the forces that make the tree grow. Problems are the movement of life, not duality.

Those on the spiritual path can also come to the point where they realize that they no longer see the obstacles as problems but as opportunities for growth, as life in movement. As long as we are on this human plane, we never surmount the ups and downs, but we can understand them in the light of truth, and they are never quite so frightening, quite so destructive, or quite so insurmountable. We deal with them as well as we can at the human level; we deal with them in our moments of quiet in the recognition of spiritual contact. The stinger is taken out of the scorpion's tail. Now our full powers are directed fruitfully in overcoming the obstacles rather than dissipated through fear and inactivity.

In life and human relationships as well as in nature, the tides ebb and flow. Casual friendships as well as the intensely personal relationships of marriage have times of ebb and times of flow. A creative relationship cannot be all flow with no ebb. A so-called perfect marriage with no reversals, no rough periods, would not be an alive and creative marriage. Just as the ebbing tide leaves shells and beautiful living things on the beach, so also the ebb of human relationships often causes the movement of life and reveals its beauty. To desire an ebbless relationship is to desire a dead one.

The ebbs and flows are only humanly dualistic. In reality there is only the one power of life or God at work. When we realize this oneness of God we can face the ebbs expectantly and creatively, waiting to see what new depths of soul they will reveal in our marriage or association.

There are those who see this double path as an excuse. They feel it gives them the liberty to use human means one minute and dismiss things as spiritual unrealities the next. Not a bit. To be a whole man we must bring all aspects to bear on all of life at all times. But we know that at any one moment, it is impossible to comprehend totally the pyramid in human terms. So we circle the pyramid until the full truth is revealed at every level.

We can look at a human situation without insulting our intelligence and realize it will bring pain and discomfort to the human lives involved. Some might call this judgment. But we, while still dealing with the problem in the picture it presents, can turn within and, with faith, know not to judge one way or the other the spiritual nature of what we see. We can know that what we behold is life in action, and the action of harmony will quite soon reveal itself.

Often the harmony appears so suddenly that man calls it a miracle. And it is a miracle, the miracle of the "word made flesh," the miracle of the life of Christ, the miracle that can free you and me. But it does not have to appear supernatural. It can be supranatural. When a man is told that he has a lung infection because there are X rays to prove it, there is no less of a miracle when, after getting inner release in prayer, it is discovered that the X ray was faulty. The fact that he now does not have the infection is just as much a miracle. Nothing changes either way but man's ignorance. And prayer can illuminate ignorance.

Whenever one heals a pimple, it is just as important a healing as that of a cancer, for it proves the principle. If the principle works for the small, it works for the big. If spirit gives you any freedom, the truth of the power of spirit is there, and it can give you complete freedom. If you have made any progress whatsoever as a person, then you have the Christ within you and can reach the height. Healing, spiritual healing, is definitely a reality and a part of life. It is also a major stumbling block for mankind. Because of failure in healing spiritually, and because of the realization of the danger of egotistical use being made of the ability, man has tried to leave healing out of religion. But healing and the truths behind it can no more be left out of a complete understanding of the spiritual life than algebra can be left out of mathematics. The whole of mathematics goes beyond algebra, but one cannot and should not leave it and its principles out of one's consciousness, if one expects to become a master mathematician. No one can leave anything out of life, bad or good, if one expects to become a master at living fully and wholly.

Spiritual healing has been lost to Christianity for so many centuries. In the past century when it was reintroduced as a solid principle and not as a freak special dispensation for a few, the pendulum swung too far in the other direction. Many believed that spiritual healing was the end in itself and sat in condemnation of all those who needed healing or who did not encompass it in their understanding. Jesus used healing and the power of spiritual truth only to demonstrate the presence of truth in man's consciousness. Because man first came to Jesus out of human needs, by filling those human needs Jesus led him to the realization that there was a principle of life to be revealed. Then He took man beyond healing.

Healing is only a part of the circle. It is a link, an important link, but only a link. God is the circle of life, love, and truth. God can only be himself. All that he is. But human beings do not want so much life. The choice is too stratospheric, too absolute for most humans. Few are ready, willing, or able to live truth that completely. For the total experience of life, of God, is beyond healing, security, or the retention of individual ego.

Faith is believing despite appearances, but it is also proceeding despite the consequences. The rebellion of man against his laws, the extreme desire to experience all of life from prison to cathedral, is further proof that we are on the edge of the great day when ultimately false death will be driven away, and man will live fully.

Until we know that in every truth the opposite also is true, that there is virtue in suffering as well as in salvation, that man is never wholly saint or sinner, that good as well as evil is man's outlook, until we realize that time and its lack of reality both exist—we are one-sided; we are not accepting total life. Only by means of time do we see a person as saint becoming sinner, or sinner becoming saint; only by time do we judge bad and good. By my oneness with all being, I am both sinner and saint, and there can be no surprise when my clay feet are apparent, when my acts reveal weakness and stumbling under the cross. Then, and only then, can we know that everything we have been through in life, and everything we have yet to go through, is necessary. Every moment of greed and fear that we have experienced was necessary to bring us to where we are. Every moment of love and truth was necessary, and all for the glory of the whole life. Without having suffered the dregs of the human enigma and defeat, we could never have known that end of the spectrum of life. Only by touching the hem of God and seeing for a moment that it is I, can I know the other end of the spectrum.

I must look out the window of life at that tree and not expect it to be anything other than that which it is. I must not love the tree because it is part of God, because it is going to flower, because it is going to give me fruit. I must not love it because God planted the seed from which it grew, or because it was any distinct size or shape in the past, or will be in the future. I must love it just because it is. I am and it is. And that is enough. Only then am I really loving.

There are those who rush around trying to force open the doors of life, and though this is not living through inner guidance, they work less harm than those who refuse to walk through the doors of life that are open to them. Through the experiences of life we gain freedom. Perhaps there is the appearance of a snake pit, of difficulty, of discomfort behind the door that life has placed before one; but perhaps on the other side of that snake pit is eternal freedom and joy. Those who cling to security are clinging to death, while those who wholly experience what life puts before them are on the way toward infinity.

The greatest love we can have for Jesus Christ is to identify with him, to experience the fullness he experienced. As we have not suffered the final crucifixion and ascension, we cannot humanly identify with that; but we can identify with his agony in the Garden of Gethsemane. Each one of us has known what it is to throw himself down and cry and ask for help. Each one of us has said, "Let this cup pass from me."

This cup is the cup of life, and we must drink from it if we expect communion and union. "He took the cup and gave it to them saying, 'drink ye all of it.'" Drink all of it. Experience the whole of life. That is what life is here for. A few verses later, in his own example of humanity, Jesus said: "Oh father, if it be possible, let this cup pass from me." He recognized the bitterness of the cup and even wanted it to pass from him individually, but he added, "Nevertheless, not as I will, but as thou wilt," and he took the next step of drinking the whole of life.

Communion is the willingness to drink all of the cup of life. Any time we turn away from life we deny communion. It means accepting even human action from which we would wish to run, as Jesus wanted to run from his actions. Saying it once was not enough, for the struggle was hard, and a few verses later he said again, "If this cup pass not from me unless I drink it, thy will be done." And there is the key. We get beyond the necessity of drinking the cup only by drinking ALL of it. We attain our oneness with absolute truth and ascend out of the level of humanness only when we have drunk all the cup. To deny the cup is to deny the body of Christ, for his body is the consciousness of the potential fullness of man. When we refuse to admit our humanity, we are rejecting the body of Christ. When we try to escape into the mind, we are denying the body of Christ. When we are afraid of sin in ourselves and in others, we are denying that God is the only power and we are rejecting the body of God. This cup of life is the very source of life.

This cup is the Holy Grail. Man has searched the world over for the Holy Grail. Only by drinking the whole cup can we realize that God is the only power, that there really is no evil, that we are transcendent, not human as we thought, but God expressed. The Holy Grail is within the grasp of each man who dares to live life fully, to live at all levels of his being at once, who dares to commune with God. Thus he communes with God.